Asperger Syndrome

A Practical Guide for Teachers

Val Cumine

Julia Leach

Gill Stevenson

David Fulton Publishers
London

David Fulton Publishers Ltd
Ormond House, 26–27 Boswell Street, London WC1N 3JZ

www.fultonpublishers.co.uk

First published in Great Britain by David Fulton Publishers 1998
Reprinted 1998 (twice), 1999 (three times), 2000 (twice), 2001

Note: The right of Val Cumine, Julia Leach and Gill Stevenson to be identified
as the authors of this work has been asserted by them in accordance with
the Copyright, Designs and Patents Act 1988.

Copyright © Val Cumine, Julia Leach and Gill Stevenson 1998

British Library Cataloguing in Publication Data
A catalogue record for this book is available from the British Library

ISBN 1–85346–499–6

Typeset by Textype Typesetters, Cambridge
Printed in Great Britain by Bell and Bain Ltd, Glasgow

Contents

Preface

This book stems from the authors' involvement in a three-year project, researching autism and Asperger syndrome in Lancashire. During that time, the authors met over 100 children with Asperger syndrome, in a variety of settings. The content of the book draws on this breadth of experience.

The anecdotes in the book are all based on real children, but names have been changed for reasons of confidentiality.

The authors met many parents of children with Asperger syndrome, but one deserves a special mention: Lynda Bannister, mother of John, who writes so eloquently and positively of her son's strengths and difficulties. We are pleased to have the opportunity to quote directly from her writings. Lynda stands as a representative of all the parents and children from whom we have learnt so much.

John – alone amongst others   *Lynda Bannister*

Chapter 1
Asperger Syndrome: An Introduction

Hans Asperger (1906–1980) lived and worked in Vienna. He qualified as a doctor and specialised in paediatrics. His work brought him into contact with a number of boys who found it difficult to 'fit in' socially. In addition to their poor social interaction skills, the boys had difficulties with the social use of language, together with a limited ability to use and understand gesture and facial expression. Also evident were repetitive, stereotypical behaviours, often with 'abnormal fixations' on certain objects.

Who was Asperger?

Having noted the similarities in the behaviour of a number of these boys, Asperger (1944) wrote and presented his paper 'Autistic psychopathies in childhood'. He recognised how severely the boys' difficulties affected their everyday lives, commenting, 'they made their parents' lives miserable and drove their teachers to despair'. He was also aware of the boys' many positive features – they often had a high level of independent thinking, together with a capacity for special achievements – but he didn't underestimate the impact of their individuality on others with whom they came into contact, and he noted their vulnerability to teasing and bullying.

Asperger's paper was written in German towards the end of World War II and for this reason reached only a limited readership. It only became widely accessible in the early 1980s when it was first translated into English and referred to by Lorna Wing in her own research into autism and related conditions. It was felt that the term 'Autistic psychopathy' sounded too negative, and 'Asperger syndrome' was suggested as a more acceptable alternative.

At the same time as Asperger was doing his research in Vienna, the child psychiatrist Leo Kanner was working in Boston, USA. He saw a similar cluster of behaviours in a number of children whom he went on to describe as 'autistic' – using the same descriptor which Asperger had used for his research group. Both Kanner and Asperger had referred to the work of Bleuler (1911) when choosing the word 'autism'. However, Bleuler had used the term to describe children who had withdrawn from participation in the social world. Kanner stressed that the children he was describing had never been participants in that social world, whilst Asperger felt that the coining of the word 'autism' was 'one of the great

Autism and Asperger syndrome

linguistic and conceptual creations in medical nomenclature'.

For Kanner, 'early childhood autism', on which he wrote his (1943) paper 'Autistic disturbance of affective contact', had a number of defining features, including:

- a profound autistic withdrawal;
- an obsessive desire for the preservation of sameness;
- a good rote memory;
- an intelligent and pensive expression;
- mutism, or language without real communicative intent;
- over-sensitivity to stimuli;
- a skilful relationship to objects.

Later researchers, particularly Lorna Wing (1981b and 1991), compared Asperger's writings to Kanner's early papers and noted significant similarities between the children being described. The key difference was that the children described by Asperger had developed grammatical speech in infancy – although the speech they had was not used for the purpose of interpersonal communication.

The core difficulties in autism and Asperger syndrome are shared. Asperger syndrome involves a more subtle presentation of difficulties. This is not to say that it is a mild form of autism – as one parent said, 'My child has mild nothing.' Asperger syndrome affects every aspect of a child's life and can cause great upset for the family.

A commonly held view is that Asperger syndrome should be regarded as a sub-category of autism – part of the wider spectrum, but with sufficient distinct features to warrant a separate label. This view is useful for educational purposes as it is generally accepted that intervention and treatment approaches for children anywhere within the autism spectrum will share the same foundation.

The term Asperger syndrome is useful in explaining to parents and teachers the root of the many problems they encounter with a child who is intellectually able, yet experiences significant social difficulties.

The triad of impairments in autism

While Asperger's paper lay undiscovered, Kanner's observations on the nature of autism were the subject of much discussion, debate and further research. Lorna Wing and Judith Gould (1979) carried out an extensive epidemiological study in the London borough of Camberwell. They concluded that the difficulties characteristic of autism could be described as a 'Triad of Impairments'.

They emphasised the fundamentally social nature of the three linked areas of difficulty:

- impairment of social interaction;
- impairment of social communication;
- impairment of social imagination, flexible thinking and imaginative play.

Wing and Gould noted that there were many children who did not exactly fit Kanner's description of 'early childhood autism', but who, nevertheless, had significant difficulties within the areas of the triad. This led Wing (1981a) to use the term 'Autistic continuum' and later (Wing 1996) 'the Autistic spectrum', allowing for a broader definition of autism based on the triad.

There is acceptance that autism is characterised by the co-occurrence of impairments in social interaction, social communication and social imagination, and diagnostic criteria are agreed on the basis of the triad.

In 1981, as a result of examining Asperger's original paper, Lorna Wing (1981a) outlined the following criteria for Asperger syndrome:

- impairment of two-way social interaction and general social ineptitude;
- speech which is odd and pedantic, stereotyped in content, but which is not delayed;
- limited non-verbal communication skills – little facial expression or gesture;
- resistance to change and enjoyment of repetitive activities;
- circumscribed special interests and good rote memory;
- poor motor coordination, with odd gait and posture and some motor stereotypies.

Whereas Asperger maintained that speech was acquired at the normal age, Wing disagreed. From her own experience, she found that half the population she would describe as having Asperger syndrome had not developed language at the normal age. Criteria developed by Christopher Gillberg (1989) were broadly similar.

Two major diagnostic instruments are currently in use by clinicians – the *Diagnostic and Statistical Manual*, 4th edition (DSM IV, American Psychiatric Association 1994) and the *International Classification of Diseases*, 10th edition (ICD10, World Health Organisation 1992) – see the appendix. Both systems base their diagnostic criteria for Asperger syndrome on the three fundamental impairments outlined within the triad. Following Asperger, they rule out early language delay, and neither includes motor coordination difficulties as a diagnostic feature.

Diagnostic criteria

In 1993, Stefan Ehlers and Christopher Gillberg published the results of research which attempted to establish the prevalence of Asperger syndrome. It had been carried out in Gothenburg and involved studying children in mainstream schools. From the numbers they identified as having Asperger syndrome, they calculated a prevalence rate of 36 per 10,000, having used criteria which allowed for the presence of some early language delay.

All prevalence studies have indicated that boys are far more likely to be affected than girls. Asperger himself had felt that it could be an exclusively male difficulty. Gillberg (1991) suggests that the ratio of boys to girls is in the region of 10:1.

Numbers of children with Asperger syndrome

3

Causes As yet, the cause of Asperger syndrome is unknown. It is unlikely that there is a single cause – rather a set of triggers, any one of which, occurring at a certain time within a chain of circumstances, can cause Asperger syndrome.

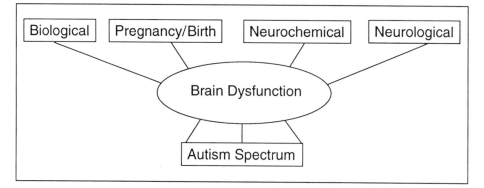

Figure 1.1 Factors which may trigger autism spectrum disorders

Asperger thought that the condition was probably transmitted genetically, describing it as an 'inherited personality disorder'. Although current thinking is that Asperger syndrome is not directly inherited, continuing research looks at the possibility of some genetic basis.

Today, Asperger syndrome is described as a brain dysfunction, and researchers are trying to pinpoint the area or areas of the brain in which the dysfunction occurs. As technology improves, it may be possible to indicate this more precisely.

Summary
- Asperger syndrome is a condition which is thought to fall within the spectrum of autism – with enough distinct features to warrant its own label.
- It was first described in 1944 by the Austrian Hans Asperger, whose work was first published in English in 1991.
- It is characterised by subtle impairments in three areas of development: social communication, social interaction and social imagination. There are, in some cases, additional motor coordination and organisational problems.
- It affects people in the average to above-average ability range.
- The prevalence is thought to be in the region of 36 per 10,000.
- Boys are more likely to be affected than girls, with a probable ratio of 10 boys to every girl.

Chapter 2

Assessment and Diagnosis

Asperger syndrome is characterised by subtle impairments in three areas of development. There are, in some cases, additional motor coordination problems. Typical features include:

Key features of Asperger syndrome

1. Social interaction

The child with Asperger syndrome:

- will be socially isolated, but may not be worried about it;
- may become tense and distressed trying to cope with the approaches and social demands of others;
- begins to realise that his peers have friendships, particularly when he reaches adolescence. He may then want friends of his own, but lack strategies for developing and sustaining friendships;
- will find it difficult to pick up on social cues;
- may behave in a socially inappropriate way – singing along to songs from 'Oliver!' is fine when you're listening to a tape, but embarrassing for your parents when you sing along during a performance at the London Palladium.

2. Social communication

The child with Asperger syndrome:

- may have superficially perfect spoken language, but it tends to be formal and pedantic. 'How do you do? My name is Jamie' may be a typical greeting from an Asperger syndrome teenager – but it is one which sets him apart from his peers, marking him out for ridicule.
- often has a voice which lacks expression. He may also have difficulty in interpreting the different tones of voice of others. Most of us can tell if someone is angry, or bored, or delighted – just from tone of voice. The child with Asperger syndrome often cannot make these judgements. This can lead to some tricky situations. One teacher had to give a student a pre-arranged visual signal, 'When I take my glasses off, you will know that I am cross with you.' Raising his voice had had no effect on the boy.
- may also have difficulty using and interpreting non-verbal communication such as: body language, gesture and facial expression.
- may understand others in a very literal way. As Grandma dried four-

year-old Ryan after his bath, she commented on his 'lovely bare feet'. Ryan became distressed and screamed, 'I'm not a bear!'

- fails to grasp the implied meanings of language. He would take a statement such as, 'It's hot in here' at face value – where the rest of us would take the hint and open a window.

3. Social imagination and flexibility of thought

The child with Asperger syndrome:

- often has an all-absorbing interest which his peers find unusual;
- may insist that certain routines are adhered to;
- is limited in his ability to think and play creatively;
- often has problems transferring skills from one setting to another.

4. Motor clumsiness

The child with Asperger syndrome:

- may be awkward and gauche in his movements;
- often has organisational problems – unable to find his way around, or collect together the equipment he needs;
- finds it hard to write and draw neatly, and tasks are often unfinished.

Case studies

Although children with Asperger syndrome have broad characteristics in common, the individual key features present in many different ways in different children. To illustrate this variety, here are six brief case studies of contrasting children. Sebastian and George are both infants, Alastair and Michael are juniors, whilst Jeff and Adrian are at secondary school.

1. Sebastian

Sebastian, a solemn-faced five year old, already had a diagnosis of semantic-pragmatic disorder. On starting school, he immediately experienced difficulties:

- He showed little interest in the other children, simply intervening in their play in order to take over the equipment, e.g., the computer.
- He couldn't stay with a partner in PE or games, and at playtime he could be found 'chugging' round the circles marked on the playground – sounding like a train.
- He wouldn't comply with his teacher's instructions.
- He would constantly ask questions in a deep stentorian tone – often when he knew the answers already.
- He would give orders to adults – 'Get it NOW!' but with no intention of being rude.

- When in the classroom, he often produced loud and uncontrolled noises which sounded like cars, whistles or bells.
- He would engage in self-directed or ritualistic activities – especially switching lights on and off and activating the fire alarm and fire extinguishers.
- He would run out of the classroom and turn the taps on in the cloakroom.
- Any imaginative play was solitary, and related to his special interests.
- There were some difficulties in PE, and he'd had occupational therapy.

At home his Mum had noted Sebastian's unusual preoccupations from an early age – shutting doors, flicking lights and a fascination for central heating pipes. He liked things to happen in a set order. For example: before he could eat a boiled egg, he had to check the egg timer, and arrange a particular spoon, plate and egg-cup in a certain way on the table.

He watched 'Thomas the Tank Engine' videos endlessly.

2. George

George, six years old, was still in a reception class.

- A passive child, he had no interest in other children.
- His preference was to complete the same form board over and over again.
- Most of his peers had given up trying to interact with him.
- A few peers would treat him cruelly – throwing a ball for him to retrieve like a dog; telling him to lick the floor in the toilets (he saw no reason not to comply).
- He had bizarre language, especially when answering questions. He would often echo what had been said.
- He had some odd facial expressions – unrelated to context.
- Reading and spelling were very good (for his age), but comprehension was poor.
- He would walk on tiptoe, flapping his hands and slapping his legs.
- He liked to have a small piece of string to 'twizzle'.

3. Alastair

Alastair, nine years old, was relatively new to his school. His previous school had seen him as a deliberately uncooperative child with behavioural difficulties.

- He found interacting with other children very difficult.
- He wanted to have friends and would approach other children, but his approaches were clumsy, perhaps pushing or kicking someone – then being surprised and distressed at the retaliation.
- He was extremely sensitive to teasing, and felt he was the sole butt of teasing.
- He found it hard to understand instructions which were given to the whole class, but couldn't seem to ask for help.
- He had great difficulty following the rules of games such as rounders.

- He often said things 'out of the blue' – unrelated to what was happening.
- He wanted his work to look perfect, and would keep rubbing a word out and writing it again – until there was a hole in the paper.
- He was frequently tense and anxious, but was unable to express his feelings.
- He found change unnerving.
- He would forget where things were stored in the classroom – even though he'd been in the same room for almost a year.

4. Michael

Michael, at eight years old, was a Year 3 child in a Year 2 class.

- He wanted to involve others in his play, but he would grab them physically, rather than asking them to join him.
- His language sounded old fashioned, other children saw him as odd and mostly avoided him.
- He was unaware of the consequences of his actions on the feelings of others. Having tied string across the stairs, he was only interested in recording how many times his brother bumped his head on the way down, unaware that it might hurt him.
- He had excellent skills with construction toys, but would never let anyone share his play.
- He was particularly fascinated by electrical wiring – without any awareness of the dangers.
- The sound of the wind would make him scream.

5. Jeff

Jeff, at age 14, was in Year 8 in an all-boys high school.

- He would become very anxious at lunchtime at the prospect of going into the noisy, bustling dining hall.
- He didn't like to be watched while he was eating. Even at home he would eat in his bedroom if visitors came.
- In group or team activities he would watch the others to see what to do, but he always seemed 'out of step'.
- He thought that some others were picking on him, and over-reacted by bringing a screwdriver to school – to 'get them'.
- He would talk endlessly about agriculture – if he could find anyone to listen.
- With poor coordination, he irritated the others in his PE class. Nobody wanted him on their team.

6. Alex

Alex, at 16 years old, had been a pupil in a residential school for children with speech and language difficulties. His Speech Therapist described him as 'an absent minded professor'.

- The 'unwritten' social rules were a closed book to Alex. He would call to his teacher across the classroom, 'She's got no idea!' – referring to his support assistant.
- In partner activities, he would ignore his partner's attempts to work with him, sometimes pushing him away.
- He was very sensitive to name calling, but was seen as eccentric by the other boys who made up a predictable nickname from Alex's surname.
- He had semantic-pragmatic language difficulties.
- He talked in a 'mid-Atlantic' accent, at high speed and full volume.
- He had comprehension difficulties, and he would question and interrupt inappropriately.
- He enjoyed talking about himself and his interests, which included: video games, watching TV, entering competitions, reading comics and using the computer.
- He had recently discovered jokes, and carried joke books around with him.
- He had unique strategies for solving Maths questions, and would become cross and confused by his teacher's attempts to teach him more regular strategies.
- He found problem solving difficult because he could not detect what strategy to apply.
- His body language was gauche, his gestures lacking in spontaneity, and his range of facial expression limited.

Assessment: background to current approaches

We try not to stick the Asperger 'label' on him like a blob on the end of his nose.　　　　　　　　　　　　　Lynda Bannister (Mother of John)

As with autism, no blood test or brain scan yet exists which can make a clear-cut diagnosis of Asperger syndrome, and children with Asperger syndrome cannot be distinguished by their physical appearance. Whilst it is accepted that autism is a development disorder of non-specific origin which is organically based, and which has pervasive psychological effects, it can still only be recognised by informed observation of behaviour. It cannot be identified by a specific behaviour, rather, it is inferred from the interpretation of a pattern of behaviours. This interpretation depends on a 'sound background of clinical knowledge' according to Uta Frith (1989), an eminent researcher in the field of autism and Asperger syndrome. Christopher Gillberg (Gillberg and Coleman 1992), who has carried out a great deal of research into the condition of Asperger syndrome, writes that 'clinical experience is a . . . fundamental element of utmost importance' in making a diagnosis, and refers to the 'gestalt acumen' of experienced clinicians which enables them to recognise the disorder despite widely varying individual presentation.

Digby Tantam (1997), a psychiatrist who has been particularly involved in the diagnosis of adolescents and adults with Asperger syndrome, encapsulates the particular difficulties in diagnosing the condition when he describes people with Asperger syndrome as 'more individual than individual'.

The case studies prior to this section serve to illustrate just how different individuals with Asperger syndrome can be from one another. Researchers have worked increasingly collaboratively to develop consistent criteria for the diagnosis of autism and Asperger syndrome. This has helped to clarify the boundaries of the conditions, but the debate continues.

A landmark in the search for diagnostic criteria which would be both necessary and sufficient to describe and specify autism came with Lorna Wing's identification of the 'triad of impairment' of social interaction in 1981. All aspects of the triad, impaired social interaction, impaired social communication, impaired play and lack of flexible thinking, combine to define autism, being present in all those with autism, and not present in this particular combination in other groups.

This definition formed the basis of the diagnostic criteria for autism in the World Classification Systems: ICD 9 (WHO 1978) and DSM III-R (American Psychiatric Association 1987). Then in 1992, for the first time, ICD 10 (WHO) gave diagnostic criteria for Asperger syndrome separately from autism. These criteria define Asperger syndrome as similar to autism, but without the language and cognitive impairments. As noted in Chapter One, however, debate continues as to whether Asperger syndrome should be regarded as part of the autism spectrum or separate from it.

Diagnosis of Asperger syndrome can involve a range of professionals. Medical diagnosis may be given by Psychiatrists, Paediatricians (either hospital or community based) or local health authority medical officers. Some Local Education Authorities (LEAs) rely on the assessment of the Educational Psychologist to determine that a child's difficulties fall within the autism spectrum and are indicative of Asperger syndrome, this being sufficient to identify approaches to educational provision and intervention. Other professionals who may contribute information relevant to the identification of the child's difficulties include Speech and Occupational Therapists and Physiotherapists, as well as teaching staff in schools and nurseries.

Differential diagnosis

Differential diagnosis is the process of deciding what the condition is – and what it isn't. It involves comparing the child's behaviour with behaviour typical of other disorders which could account for the same symptoms.

Jonathan Green (1990), a child and adolescent psychiatrist who has researched the nature of Asperger syndrome, outlines several areas for differential diagnosis. He points out that the differential diagnosis of children who may have Asperger syndrome involves considering alternative conditions in which some of the features are similar to those of the triad of impairments.

These include the following:

Ordinary insensitivity

Asperger (1944) saw the condition as an extreme form of male intelligence, indicating that the characteristic social insensitivity was at the end of a continuum of normal behaviour. However, as Green (1990) points out, there is evidence that this is not the case. In studies comparing children with Asperger syndrome to other child psychiatry patients with social difficulties, only the Asperger syndrome group showed 'odd and bizarre speech, gesture and facial expression'.

Emotional disorder

Children with emotional difficulties, perhaps due to family and social circumstances, may present as unusually withdrawn and uncommunicative. However, they will usually respond more quickly to treatment and intervention (Green *op. cit.*).

Dyspraxia

Children with Asperger syndrome are often clumsy, with poorly developed fine-motor and eye-hand coordination skills. Conversely, some children with severe dyspraxia also experience marked social problems. Therefore, differential diagnosis can be difficult in some cases, particularly with younger children. However, the distinction is important because children whose problems are fundamentally associated with dyspraxia will respond more readily to social-skills-based intervention because of a relatively intact ability to form social relationships. They are also less rigid and obsessional in their interests than children with Asperger syndrome. In terms of educational intervention, there will be areas of similarity, but the priorities will be different.

Language disorder

The borders of developmental language disorders and autism can be difficult to define. When children are able to compensate for language difficulties by using gesture, facial expression, mime and signs, it will be clear that that the source of difficulty is language-based. However, as Rutter (1978) observed, some children present a mixed picture. Social, communication and behavioural difficulties may be observed in young children with severe receptive language disorders as well as in young children with autism spectrum disorders. Collaboration between professionals involved in assessment (e.g., Speech and Language Therapists, Psychologists and Paediatricians) is essential. As the child reaches school age, the picture is usually becoming clearer.

Attention Deficit Hyperactivity Disorder (ADHD)

Young children with ADHD will evidence many behaviours which may also be present in Asperger syndrome, for example: not seeming to listen when spoken to directly; not following through on instructions; experiencing difficulty organising tasks and activities; talking excessively; interrupting and being easily distracted. Occasionally, young children of five or six years of age with Asperger syndrome may initially be diagnosed as having ADHD, possibly being prescribed medication and being given appropriate behavioural intervention. Usually in the case of ADHD, prescribed medication, together with appropriate behavioural and social skills intervention, will bring about rapid improvement in social functioning. If, however, social difficulties remain and are resistant to change, the differential diagnosis of Asperger syndrome may need to be considered.

Other psychiatric disorders

On occasion, children with bizarre patterns of behaviour and unusual thought processes will be given other psychiatric diagnoses, for example: 'schizoid personality', 'obsessive-compulsive disorder'. The social impairments in such conditions are not those of Asperger syndrome. In such cases it is essential that a child psychiatrist is involved.

Multi-disciplinary assessment

It is evident that the multifaceted nature of the difficulties and impairments of Asperger syndrome may require involvement in diagnosis and intervention from a variety of professionals working within different services. The needs of both child and family will best be served by an awareness amongst all the professionals of the range of skills and expertise which it may be useful to deploy at an early stage in the process of assessment and identification.

Approaches to assessment

Assessment of children where Asperger syndrome is under consideration should first and foremost be based on:

- a thorough knowledge of the autism spectrum, the triad of impairments and the nature of Asperger syndrome;
- a thorough understanding of psychological explanations for the underlying impairments in Asperger syndrome;
- an awareness of the extremely individual presentation of the characteristic impairments in Asperger syndrome;
- Knowledge of the diagnostic criteria for Asperger syndrome in ICD 10 and DSM IV.

This background knowledge can then be used to prompt:

- careful and sensitive gathering of information;
- informed observation;
- the selection of situation and context;
- the staging of appropriate interactive events, selection of tasks and useful assessment procedures and materials.

In the process of assessment, rating scales developed for use with children with autism spectrum disorders may be used. Examples include the following:

The Autism Diagnostic Interview (ADI) (Le Couteur *et al.* 1989)

This is a standardised interview developed as a research tool for use with parents. The areas of the triad are given extremely detailed coverage, with care being taken to present open-ended questions and probes for information which do not bias the answers elicited. Specialised training at the Rutter Institute is required. An algorithm is provided to aid diagnosis for those using this procedure.

The Autism Diagnostic Observation Schedule (ADOS) (Lord *et al.* 1989)

This procedure, for use in individual assessment, involves the presentation of a series of activities requiring social interaction, the use of imagination, playskills and the ability to explain feelings. Again, a diagnostic algorithm is used and professional training is required.

The Childhood Autism Rating Scale (CARS) (Schopler *et al.* 1980)

This rating scale, devised in North Carolina for use in the TEACCH (Treatment and Education of Autistic and Communication Handicapped Children) clinic, relies on a comprehensive set of observations based on several diagnostic systems. Evidence is gained for all 15 items which reflect many facts of autism. The rating scale is summative.

The Psychoeducational Profile – Revised (PEP-R) (Schopler *et al.* 1990)

This assessment involves presenting the child with a series of activities covering an inventory of behaviours and skills relevant to autism, and is designed to identify uneven and idiosyncratic learning patterns. Developmental skills are assessed in seven areas, and atypical

Diagnostic and assessment tools for use within the autism spectrum

behaviours in a further four areas. The resulting profile is used to help design individual education programmes for children.

These instruments are reliable in discriminating children with autism from those with severe learning difficulties and from normally developing children from the age of three years onwards. However, they are less sensitive in areas where the finest discrimination is required, for example: in differentiating language disorders or mild Asperger syndrome. As yet, there is no established rating scale for use specifically with children suspected of having Asperger syndrome.

Qualitative assessment

While diagnostic and assessment tools such as these are useful, qualitative assessment remains crucial in the identification of Asperger syndrome, and in detailing the special educational needs which arise from it.

Such assessment will take account of functioning in and examine the interface between the areas of:

- social interaction;
- social communication;
- social imagination, flexible thinking and play;
- cognitive ability;
- developmental skills in areas such as attention control, language levels, fine- and gross-motor functioning and independence skills.

Assessment should also always include:

- a thorough developmental history;
- background medical information;
- information from any therapeutic intervention undertaken;
- educational history;
- current educational attainments.

Assessment should include information from, and observation within a range of settings:

- home and family based;
- school, nursery or playgroup setting;
- within specialist settings, e.g., Child Development Centre.

Assessment should be carried out over a period of time, since behaviour can vary from day to day as well as in different settings and with different people.

Teaching contribution to assessment and diagnosis in Asperger syndrome

While it would be inappropriate for teachers to 'go solo' in identifying, assessing, or offering a diagnosis of Asperger syndrome for a child in the educational setting, the class teacher has an important role to play in the assessment process. Frequently, it is the teacher who is the first to notice behaviour which may seem odd, unusual or different compared to that of peers. The child may be placed on Stages 1 to 3 of the Code of Practice and an Individual Education Plan (IEP) will need to be drawn up. Collaboration with external agencies may lead to a request for more specialist information, for example from the educational psychologist. If formal assessment of the child's special educational needs is undertaken, teaching staff will be expected to provide educational advice on the child.

In addition to the usual information collated on a child's educational attainments and his response to teaching, it will be helpful if the teacher gathers information regarding the child's functioning, skill levels and aspects of behaviour in areas which are particularly relevant to the assessment and diagnosis of Asperger syndrome, i.e., in the areas of social interaction, social communication and social imagination and flexible thinking.

Social interaction

Judging the extent to which the child is able to:

- use gesture, body posture, facial expression and eye-to-eye gaze in one-to-one and in group interaction, e.g., standing an appropriate distance away from others;
- appreciate social cues, given by adults or children, in one-to-one or large group conditions;
- develop peer friendships – do they play alone, or have they some ability to initiate or respond to interaction?
- share an activity with other children or adults;
- seek comfort or affection when distressed, or offer comfort to others;
- share in others' enjoyment and pleasure;
- show different responses to different people and in different settings;
- imitate other children and adults;
- respond to social praise or criticism.

Social communication

Judging the extent to which the child is able to:

- respond when called by name;
- follow verbal instructions, one-to-one or in small or large groups;
- take turns in conversation;
- initiate conversation, change topics, maintain an appropriate topic;
- be aware of the listener's needs and give non-verbal signals that he is listening;
- change topic and style of conversation to suit the listener;
- vary the tone and projection of voice according to the situation;
- recognise and respond to non-verbal cues, e.g., raised eyebrows, smile;
- understand implied meanings;
- tell or write an imaginative story;
- give a sequence of events or tell a simple story;
- give simple, ordered instructions.

Social imagination and flexible thinking

Judging the extent to which the child is able to:

- have a range of interests, and an ability to share them – as opposed to having all-absorbing, exclusive interests;
- change his behaviour according to the situation;
- accept changes in routines, rules or procedures;
- play imaginatively – alone or cooperatively;
- accept others' points of view;
- generalise learning or generate skills across the curriculum;
- plan, e.g., in the assembly of equipment, sorting out the steps of a task;
- suggest possible explanations of events;
- use inference and deduction in an academic or social context.

Observation should be carried out in a range of settings, including informal and non-academic contexts, e.g.:

- Playtime, lunch breaks, noting:
    - the extent to which their play is solitary;
    - whether they seem anxious when others approach them;
    - their level of cooperative/imaginative play.
- Cloakrooms, arrival and home-times, noting:
    - how they leave or greet their parent/carer/teacher/peers;
    - their self-help/independence skills.
- PE, noting:
    - their ability to get changed independently;
    - how well they find/work with a partner;
    - their level of participation in team games;
    - their motor and coordination skills.
- Class 'performances', e.g., Harvest Festival, class assembly, noting their ability:
    - to take on a role;
    - to project their voice for the audience;
    - to take turns;
    - wait and listen to others.

Additional opportunities for observation will present themselves during classroom activities. The use of the questionnaire in Chapter Six will help in forming an assessment of the child's functioning, and in devising individual teaching programmes.

Summary

- There is no simple test, marker or checklist which will confirm the diagnosis of Asperger syndrome.
- The presence of Asperger syndrome is inferred on the basis of interpretation of a pattern of behaviours.
- The 'boundaries' of Asperger syndrome overlap other conditions, and an awareness of the issues of differential diagnosis is essential.

- Adequate assessment and diagnosis of Asperger syndrome will involve a range of professionals from various disciplines.
- Teachers and educational support staff can provide vital and specific information to aid in the assessment process.
- Specialised tools exist which may help in the assessment process, but the role of qualitative, observation-based assessment is crucial.

Chapter 3

Educational Implications of Current Theories

As educationalists, it is our responsibility in teaching children to:

- recognise patterns of strengths and weaknesses;
- build upon strengths;
- generate effective intervention strategies.

How are we to do this for the child with Asperger syndrome?

In recent years, in the wake of the 1978 Warnock Report and the 1981 and 1993 Education Acts, there has been a movement away from 'labelling' children and, therefore, from paying much attention to a child's 'diagnosis' when planning intervention. The behaviourist school of thought has also promoted an emphasis on intervention at the level of observable behaviours and consequences.

In our experience with children with Asperger syndrome however, we have found that the 'label' or 'diagnosis' is crucial.

In order to provide effective education for children with Asperger syndrome, it is essential to understand the nature of the impairments, the sources of the difficulties, the areas of strength – in effect, the cognitive style.

To attempt to alter and modify individual behaviours in a piecemeal fashion with children with Asperger syndrome is a strategy which has major shortcomings. This is the stage we were at in the teaching of children with autism until relatively recently. There was recognition that autism is an organically based disorder characterised by a range of identifiable behaviours. The 'missing link' was at the level of psychological functioning.

The shift in emphasis in our understanding of the nature of the difficulties in autism occurred as the triad of impairments was identified, pinpointing the underlying social deficit. Previously, the difficulties of language and behaviour in autism were assumed to cause the social difficulties. Now, the difficulty in social interaction and understanding is seen to underpin the difficulty in communication and to cause many of the difficulties in behaviour.

The effort to explain the sources of social difficulty at the psychological level has led to a number of powerful models of the child's psychological functioning, powerful in their ability to generate approaches to assessment and intervention.

An ability we all appear to have, which is so commonplace as to have escaped specific investigation until relatively recently, is the ability to think about other people's thinking – and, further, to think about what they think about our thinking – and, even further, to think about what they think we think about their thinking, and so on . . . This ability underlies much of our interaction with others, informing our understanding of others' behaviour and influencing our actions towards others.

In psychological terms, this is described as the ability to appreciate that other people have mental states: intentions, needs, desires and beliefs, which may be different to our own. The term given to this ability is 'Theory of Mind'.

In 1985, a group of research psychologists (Baron-Cohen, Leslie and Frith) proposed that people with autism lack a 'Theory of Mind'. In 1990, Baron-Cohen went on to describe this as a form of 'Mind Blindness'. It was suggested that this basic cognitive deficit in autism constrains children to a deviant path of development, and that this, in turn, gives rise to complex surface behaviours.

The experiment designed to reveal the characteristic deficits of 'Theory of Mind' in autism is now quite famous and is known as 'The Sally/Anne test'. It was designed by Simon Baron-Cohen in 1985 to test the prediction that children with autism would lack the ability to understand beliefs.

The experiment was carried out:

- with children with autism with mental ages above four years;
- with a control group of children with Down's Syndrome who also had mental ages above four years;
- with normally developing four-year-old children.

In the Sally/Anne test, Sally and Anne are two dolls. Sally has a basket and Anne has a box. In the story, which is acted out in front of the child, Sally puts a marble into her basket while Anne is watching. She then leaves to go for a walk. While she is away, Anne puts Sally's marble into her own box. Sally returns from her walk and wants to play with her marble. The child subject is then asked, 'Where will Sally look for her marble?' The correct answer is, 'In her basket', for that is where Sally left her marble, and where she believes it still is. Children with autism answer that Sally will look, 'In the box', because that is where the marble actually is – even though Sally has not seen Anne taking it from the basket and placing it in the box. This contrasts with the children in the control groups who give the correct answer.

Many further experiments have been carried out examining this area of functioning and the evidence is that whereas most young children can pass this sort of test by the age of four years, even the more able children with autism do not master the task until a later age. Uta Frith (1991) tested 50 able children with autism and found that no child passed 'Theory of Mind' tasks with a chronological age of under eleven years and a mental age of under five years.

In children with Asperger syndrome, 'Theory of Mind' still constitutes an area of difficulty. The more able children do come to an

'Mind Blindness' and the 'Theory of Mind' impairment

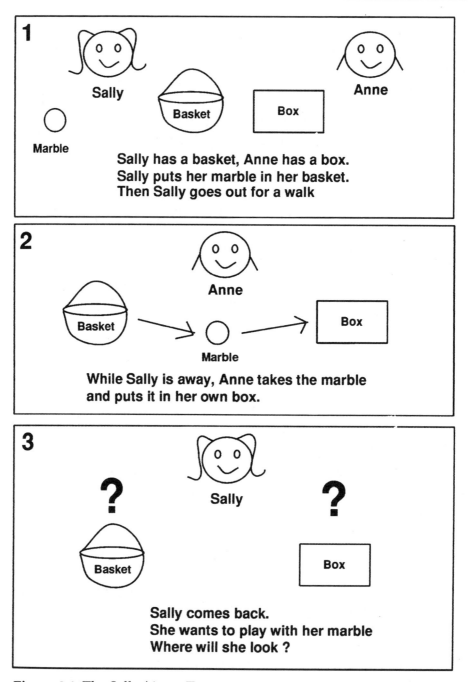

Figure 3.1 The Sally/Anne Test

understanding, although this is at a much later stage than in the normally developing child. Happé and Frith (1995) suggest that this is between the ages of 9–14 years, in contrast to four years in normal development.

It appears that the route to developing an understanding of other minds, and even an awareness that other people do have minds is much more difficult for people with Asperger syndrome, and can be likened, in degree of severity, to the difficulties involved in learning to read for the dyslexic child. In contrast, for the rest of us it is so effortless that we feel that we were born with it. Even when a basic level of understanding is reached, the young person with Asperger syndrome may not manage to reach the next stage of understanding, that is that people not only have thoughts and feelings, but they can reflect on these, i.e., have thoughts and feelings about their own and other people's thoughts and feelings.

The ability of children with Asperger syndrome to perform the 'Theory of Mind' task can be investigated in practical situations in the classroom. An alternative experiment to the Sally/Anne test which can easily be replicated, is the Smarties test (Perner *et al.* 1989). In this, the child is shown a Smarties tube and asked what he thinks it contains. Upon answering 'Smarties' the child is then shown the contents of the tube – a pencil. He is then asked what another child will say if shown the tube and asked the same question. Typically, the child with Asperger syndrome will answer, 'A pencil'. Even when the next child is brought in and gets the answer wrong, the child with Asperger syndrome will fail to see the point, the 'joke' as it were. This procedure can be adapted using ordinary classroom materials. For example, a familiar crayon tub is emptied – out of the child's view – and the crayons replaced by lego bricks, and questions asked as above.

Implications of the 'Theory of Mind' impairment

The effects of the 'Theory of Mind' impairment in children with Asperger syndrome are pervasive, subtle and specific. Jordan and Powell (1995) have highlighted the implications of this impairment.

Some examples of these difficulties as they are presented in Asperger syndrome are detailed as follows:

- **Difficulty in predicting others' behaviour, leading to a fear and avoidance of other people.** Thus there will be a preference for activities which do not depend on other people, or even require the involvement of others.
- **Difficulty in reading the intentions of others and understanding the motives behind their behaviour.** Oliver, a young teenager, was quite willing (prompted by other boys) to type out salacious remarks on the school word processor. He circulated copies and even read them out to the teacher. He was so pleased to have the boys' attention and be able to make them laugh. He thought they were now his friends.
- **Difficulty in explaining own behaviour.** One young man in a school for children with emotional and behavioural difficulties alleged that a teacher had assaulted him, deliberately pushing him into a pile of chairs. He failed to say that he had been balanced on the back of a chair himself at the time, refusing to climb down – pushing the teacher away from him. When this was pointed out, he protested indignantly, 'It was obvious, it was obvious!'
- **Difficulty in understanding emotions – their own and those of others, leading to a lack of empathy.** Jake, a primary school child, would cry if he was upset, but would then try to push the tears back in – confused by his own feelings. Craig, in an infant Language Unit, stopped in the middle of a tearful outburst to squint at the tears glistening on his lashes, his attention caught by this strange phenomenon. An older boy, a teenager, developing some awareness of his difficulties when upset and angry would run to his support

assistant saying, 'Tell me what I'm feeling, tell me, tell me!'

- **Difficulty understanding that behaviour affects how others think or feel, leading to a lack of conscience, of motivation to please.** Michael used to tie string across the staircase for his brother to trip over. He was unaware of the pain and injury this could cause – he just wanted to count how many times the brother bumped his head on the way down. In the classroom, the child with Asperger syndrome does not 'pick up' the idea of paying attention to the teacher when she is speaking – or at least pretending to – as most children do in order to conform to teacher expectation.

- **Difficulty taking into account what other people know or can be expected to know, leading to pedantic or incomprehensible language.** Either no background information is given, so that the listener has no idea of what the subject of the conversation is, or every detail is given to the point of boring the listener completely.

- **Inability to read and react to the listener's level of interest in what is being said.** An obsessional interest may be talked about endlessly. Alex, at the age of 16, had recently discovered jokes. He carried several joke books around in his bag, reading out jokes repeatedly – regardless of the listener's mood or interest.

- **Inability to anticipate what others might think of one's actions.** Derek had just started at High school and had gone to the Baths with his class. He found that his swimming trunks were inside out. He went into the public area to ask his teacher for help – unaware of the effect of his nakedness on those around him.

- **Inability to deceive or to understand deception.** The teacher comes into the classroom to find that someone has played a prank and hidden the chalk. She asks who has done it. Martin tells her the culprit's name without hesitation.

- **No sharing of attention, leading to idiosyncratic reference.** A teacher, leading a group activity in an Infant class, holds up a picture of a farmyard. The focus of all the children is on the different farm animals – except for one child. Marcus, who is fascinated by electricity pylons, notices a tiny pylon in the background of the picture, and can focus on nothing else.

- **Lack of understanding of social interaction, leading to difficulties with turn-taking, poor topic maintenance in conversation, and inappropriate use of eye contact.** One young man had observed the frequency of eye contact amongst other people and asked, 'Why do people pass messages with their eyes?'

- **Difficulty in understanding 'pretend', and differentiating fact from fiction.** A diligent teacher and support assistant spent two years teaching Aaron, an able junior school pupil, the nature of stories. Eventually, the penny dropped, 'Oh! You mean it's not true!'

All of these difficulties which arise from the 'Theory of Mind' impairment affect the child's ability to interact socially in the classroom, and in the wider school environment. They influence not only his behaviour but also his thinking and thus his ability to benefit from the school curriculum.

Hobson (1993) believes the difficulties associated with 'Theory of Mind' originate at a much earlier stage in development. He holds that human capacities for social interaction are based on certain innate abilities. Difficulties in 'Theory of Mind', he postulates, arise from the infant's 'lack of basic perceptual-affective abilities and propensities that are required for a person to engage in "personal relatedness with others"'. In order for intersubjective understanding to begin at all, infants have to have an ability to respond naturally with feelings to the feelings, expressions, gestures and actions of others. They must have biologically given, 'prewired' capacities for direct perception of others' emotions and attitudes in order to begin to develop an understanding of *others* as separate beings with their own feelings, thoughts, beliefs and attitudes. And also, of course, to recognise *themselves* as beings with feelings, thoughts, beliefs and attitudes – and to realise that there is common ground, though each of us views it from a different angle.

The concept of a person is 'logically prior to that of an individual consciousness' and it is this concept, Hobson argues, which is missing in autism.

Several other theorists have suggested related explanations for the difficulties in autism. Most notably in terms of educational implications Jordan and Powell (1995), who propose that the difficulties in autism might derive from the failure to develop 'an experiencing self'. They note that children with autism have difficulties in developing a personal memory for events (personal episodic memory). That is, they have difficulty in experiencing events subjectively and then in being able to recall these events without effort – an ability most of us take for granted. When we wish to recall an event, we tend to ask ourselves, 'What was I doing? Where was I? Who was with me?' Ironically, although children with Asperger syndrome are often described as 'egocentric', real egocentricity as we understand it in our non-autistic day-to-day lives, seems to be lacking.

The implications for teachers of this lack of a sense of experiencing self are that the child will need a structure which will cue him into the salient points. The child's role in the learning process will need to be highlighted, drawn to his attention visually and verbally as Powell and Jordan (1997) suggest, using photographs, videos and prompt scripts. They point to the interrelatedness of emotions and thinking in normal development which leads us to attach 'meaning' to events. Without this personally experienced meaningfulness of events, children with autistic difficulties learn 'from the outside in', as it were, by rote and mechanistically.

The challenge to teaching presented by Powell and Jordan is that of explicit teaching of meaning – the child's attention must be drawn explicitly to how new information affects the way in which he understands the world. In this sense, transferability of knowledge becomes a process that needs to be directly taught rather than assumed.

'Theory of Mind' developments: The role of emotion and the sense of self

Principles of intervention: teaching points

Teachers and others working with children with Asperger syndrome will need to be aware of the following points:

- Dealing with surface behaviours is not enough to correct fundamental deficits.
- It is difficult to teach levels of social and personal awareness that we ourselves did not have to 'learn'.
- Learning the social skills necessary for the classroom and playground is an extremely demanding and stressful task for the child with Asperger syndrome. There may not be much 'space' left for dealing with academic tasks. Conversely, academic tasks may provide 'relief' from the stress of social interaction.
- There will be a need to specifically teach the basic social skills of listening and not interrupting; pausing to allow others a turn; sharing equipment; waiting in lines; working in small groups.
- The child will need help to recognise the effects of his actions on others and to change his behaviour accordingly.
- Beware of assuming that the child's language level represents his communication level. There will be a need to check the child's understanding.
- Be explicit when giving instructions, don't assume that the context will help to make the meaning clear.
- Assess the child's ability to use language socially, and specifically teach such skills as initiating a dialogue, listening to replies, following up with an appropriate response.
- Strategies to develop the child's self-concept, self-image and self-reference will need to be built in.
- Teach the child to identify emotions as physical, visual, auditory expressions, but also 'in situ', drawing attention to the emotional expressions of others.
- Ensure that the child is giving attention to the topic, subject or activity which is meant to be the focus of attention.
- Alert the child to his role in tasks, situations and events; use strategies to prompt the development of a personal memory.
- Beware of assuming that the 'meaning' of any task, situation, activity or event is clear to the child: relate the meaning, where possible, to the perspective he is taking.
- Draw the child's attention to the use of gesture, facial expression, eye direction, proximity in social interaction to convey attitudes and meaning.
- Make the child aware of himself as a problem solver, using visual and auditory means to promote self-reflection and recognition of self-experience.
- Don't assume the child will be able to 'read' your intentions from your behaviour.
- The child will need to learn that other people have feelings, thoughts, beliefs and attitudes and to become aware of his own thinking, feelings, beliefs and attitudes.
- Teach 'pretending' and help the child discriminate between pretence and reality.

Another theory put forward to account for the impairments in autism is that of the Central Coherence Deficit.

Central Coherence Deficit

Uta Frith, in 1989, suggested that some aspects of functioning in autism cannot be explained by 'Theory of Mind' impairment alone – for example, the insistence on sameness, attention to detail rather than the whole, insistence on routine, obsessional preoccupations, and the existence of special skills.

Research findings indicated that children with autism performed better than would be expected on the Children's Embedded Figures Test, and on the Block Design Test (a sub-test of the Wechsler Intelligence Scales for Children – WISC, Wechsler 1991). The Children's Embedded Figures Test (CEFT, Witkin *et al.* 1971) involves spotting a hidden figure, e.g., a triangle, in a larger drawing, e.g., a pram. The Block Design Test requires the child to assemble individual segmented blocks to match a given drawing of a whole, which involves first breaking up the whole design into its constituent parts.

Frith argued that in autism, the problem with these tasks was not in overcoming the tendency to see the picture as a whole but in the failure to see the whole picture in the first place. The advantage shown by children with autism is thus attributed specifically to their ability to see parts over wholes. Interestingly, as Francesca Happé (1994) points out, Kanner in 1943 saw as one of the universal features of autism the 'inability to experience wholes without full attention to the constituent parts'. He had also commented on the tendency to fragmentary processing and the children's resistance to change: 'a situation, a performance, a sentence is not regarded as complete if it is not made up of exactly the same elements that were present at the time the child was first confronted with it'.

Frith (1989) describes 'central coherence' as the tendency to draw together diverse information to construct higher-level meaning in context. In individuals who process information normally, there is a tendency to make sense of situations and events according to their context. In individuals with Asperger syndrome this does not occur.

Five-year-old Ben, sitting in the interview room with his reading folder on his knee, was asked by the psychologist to 'take your book out'. He got up and left the room with it. The same little boy later read a whole story involving grumbling children taking all their old toys to a jumble sale at their parents' instruction. Subsequently, given their pocket money, the children buy back all their toys, arriving home to their parents' looks of consternation. Ben completely missed the point of the story, even though he could identify the pictures in which the children and the parents looked sad or happy, and relate what happened to the toys. He showed real interest though in the appearance of a fan in the corner of several of the pictures.

When Ryan protested, 'I'm not a bear!' to his grandmother's comment on his 'lovely bare feet', he was making a similar mistake.

Implications of the Central Coherence Deficit

Some of the difficulties which can be expected to occur when there is difficulty recognising wholes, in making sense of events in context and preference for detail include:

- **Idiosyncratic focus of attention.** The child will not necessarily focus on what you as the teacher may consider to be the obvious focus of attention, or point of the task.
- **Imposition of own perspective.** What appears prominent to the child will determine his perspective on the learning situation. William was fascinated by knights and castles. His teacher led a group discussion on the topic of faces, and gave him collage materials to construct a face picture. William used the pieces to assemble a picture of a castle!
- **Preference for the known.** Without the ability to quickly see the point, and 'get the drift' of others' actions and communications, the child with Asperger syndrome will feel safer sticking to known procedures and established routines.
- **Inattentiveness to new tasks.** As a teacher, you will find it difficult to enthuse a pupil with Asperger syndrome by talking of new, exciting and interesting ideas, as their potential appeal will not be recognised.
- **Difficulty in choosing and prioritising.** Without a guiding principle or superordinate goal, the child with Asperger syndrome has difficulty in choosing and prioritising. Jake, when asked to choose the sweets he wanted, constructed a complex chart that listed categories of sweets and brand names before he could decide whether to have Rolos, Wine Gums or Polo Mints.
- **Difficulty in organising self, materials, experiences.** Again, without a guiding principle or overall plan, the child with Asperger syndrome often has difficulty in all matters of organisation. He may be unable to find the Art paper in a familiar classroom; to find his way round school in time for the next lesson; or to equip his school bag with the books and pens he is likely to need. In fact, the school bag has been kicked and blamed for not yielding up its contents more efficiently (on more than one occasion).
- **Difficulty seeing connections and generalising skills and knowledge.** Children with Asperger syndrome may show great aptitude in one area of knowledge, but be unable to generalise this in a variety of situations. Clyde has tremendous ability in Maths, able to calculate three-figure multiplication in his head at age nine years. However, when his teacher gave the class a test involving different presentations of the sums, Clyde became angry and anxious, crying, 'You didn't teach me these, I can't do them.'
- **Lack of compliance.** For the teacher with a class of 30 or more children, this is probably the most taxing aspect of this difficulty. Aidan spent the first two years of his schooling wandering about the classroom and school at will, talking at length in an American accent – seemingly unaware of the requirement to stay with his class group. He baffled his teachers with his apparent insouciance.

Again, all of these difficulties which arise from the proposed Central Coherence Deficit affect the child's ability to integrate into his class group in school. They restrict the child's ability to cooperate with, or even, simply, to notice the demands of others – affecting not only behaviour, but also thinking, and thus the ability to benefit from the school curriculum.

Teachers and others working with children with Asperger syndrome will need to be aware of the following points:

- Make the beginning and end points of tasks clear, e.g., using a list of steps to task completion, or a series of prompt cards, pictures or diagrams.
- Consider using a model or picture of the final goal or end product, so that the child knows what is expected.
- Avoid ambiguity, use visual clues to highlight meaning.
- Specifically teach the child how to make choices.
- Build in opportunities for the child to generalise knowledge and skills.
- Make the connections with previous skills or knowledge explicit.
- Teach stories using sequences of picture cards. Draw the child's attention to cause and effect, motives and plot.

Principles of intervention: teaching points

Executive function is defined as 'the ability to maintain an appropriate problem-solving set for attainment of a future goal' (Luria 1966). Sally Ozonoff gives this definition in her 1995 paper, proposing deficits in executive functioning as the central deficit in autism. Executive functioning is mediated by the frontal lobes of the brain and one hypothesis is that this area of the brain guides behaviour by mental representations or 'inner models of reality' (Goldman-Rakic 1987).

Executive function behaviours include:

- planning;
- self-monitoring;
- inhibition of prepotent, correct responses;
- behavioural flexibility;
- organised search;
- set maintenance and change.

Executive Function Deficit

Ozonoff points out how these functions are often impaired in people with autism and Asperger syndrome. The behaviour of people with autism is often rigid, inflexible and perseverative. They are often impulsive, having difficulty holding back a response. They may have a large store of knowledge, but have trouble applying this knowledge meaningfully. They often seem narrowly focused on detail, and cannot see the whole 'picture'.

Implications of Executive Function Deficit

Some of the implications of Executive Function Deficit include:

- **Difficulties in perceiving emotion.** There is an inability to hold images of the different forms of expression internally. The person with autism or Asperger syndrome is guided by the external appearance of the face or the perceptual pattern, so that an open mouth can equally be an expression of fear or surprise. (The perceptual pattern thus dominating and determining the response is described as 'prepotent'.)
- **Difficulties in imitation.** Similarly, there is a need to hold an image of the other's behaviour in mind long enough to be able to imitate it.
- **Difficulties in pretend play.** In order to pretend, external objects in the environment have to be held in mind, then transformed or represented (re-presented) as something else.

The difficulty with Executive Function Deficit theory as a primary explanation of autism impairments is that children with other developmental difficulties also evidence executive function impairments, for example: attention deficit disorder and conduct disorder.

However, the implications in terms of the children's behaviour may include:

- **Difficulty in planning.** Children with Asperger syndrome will often appear incapable of organising an approach to a task.

Alan had been in the same classroom for nearly a year, but when asked to go and get some paper, he meandered into the centre of the classroom, then stood, looking lost.

Craig, in the nursery for 18 months, was asked to hand round the biscuits. He could not see where to start, and how to get from one table to another. When he got to the second table (where his own seat was), he sat down – taking a biscuit for himself, and eating it.

- **Difficulty in starting and stopping.** Very often, the child with Asperger syndrome will sit at the desk or table, all his work in front of him, but seemingly unable or unwilling to start the task. A little help getting started, perhaps a physical prompt, will often be all that is necessary. Once he gets going, however, he may perseverate, unclear as to when the task is finished.

Principles of intervention: teaching points

Teachers and others working with children with Asperger syndrome will need to be aware of the following points:

- break tasks down into clearly identifiable steps;
- develop a hierarchy of sub-goals;
- sequence activities towards the goals.

To enable the child to consolidate and apply knowledge, the child will need help to:

- identify the main idea in new information;
- draw associations between new knowledge and already acquired knowledge;
- see the whole 'picture' rather than focus on details.

Summary

Before planning educational intervention for the child with Asperger syndrome, it is important to understand the child at the psychological level.

Current psychological theories which extend our understanding of children with autism and Asperger syndrome propose that these children have impairments in 'Theory of Mind', Central Coherence and Executive Function. An understanding of these theories leads to an understanding of their educational implications.

Chapter 4
Educational Intervention

Hans Asperger felt that educational 'training' would help the child, and for the majority of children this has proved to be the case. To be effective, intervention for children with Asperger syndrome must be grounded in an understanding of the nature of the condition and its fundamental impairments.

Allowance needs to be made for individuality as no two children are affected in exactly the same way.

A framework for educational intervention

Asperger syndrome has a relatively low incidence. This can make it difficult to ensure a coordinated approach and consistency of provision across a Local Education Authority (LEA).

One LEA developed a county-wide network of support, designed to meet the needs of children with autism and Asperger syndrome. This network was based on the following elements:

- a shared understanding of autism and Asperger syndrome;
- educational provision preceded by quality assessment;
- county-wide availability of specialist advice;
- careful selection and training of support teachers and assistants;
- professional links between specialist schools and mainstream schools, and between professionals from different agencies.

Although intervention may appear to be specialist, it does not necessarily mean that the child with Asperger syndrome has to attend a specialist school. It is possible to *take the specialism to the child* and enrich the mainstream situation so that, through understanding and differentiation, the child is part of the community of the school and is valued as an individual within this community.

Key roles in an ideal support network are those of the class teacher, the support teacher and the Special Support Assistant.

The role of the class teacher

The role of the class teacher is central to the education of the child with Asperger syndrome. The role can be likened to that of an orchestral conductor, pivotal in keeping everything together and 'in tune'. It is their job to ensure that all children in the class are educated at a level appropriate to their needs. To do this, it is necessary to create an environment that encourages the valuing of individuals and recognises their different learning styles. This is based on having an understanding of the needs of all the children – including the child with Asperger syndrome.

Particular areas on which the class teacher will focus are:

- creating a calm working environment;
- ensuring that the structure of the classroom is clearly laid out;
- modifying tasks to harness and build on the child's strengths;
- making sure that the child understands what is expected of him;
- introducing choice gradually, encouraging decision making;
- grading tasks, gradually increasing demands on the child;
- directing the child's attention at an individual level, rather than relying on whole class instructions;
- accessing available training;
- planning IEPs;
- recording and monitoring progress;
- evaluating intervention strategies;
- working closely with the available support network;
- establishing and maintaining home/school links.

While this may at first appear to be a challenging set of expectations, it is really just an example of good classroom practice.

An important thought to keep in mind is that the child with Asperger syndrome is part of the whole school community and should be accepted and supported by the whole school community.

The role of the support teacher

The support teacher is well placed to bring specialist understanding of Asperger syndrome into the mainstream classroom. A large part of the role is to increase the confidence of all those involved in the education of the child with Asperger syndrome. This includes boosting the confidence of the child himself and that of his parents. If all concerned feel positive, then the priority, particularly if any difficulties are met, will be to move forward and find solutions.

The effective support teacher will have:

- a thorough understanding of Asperger syndrome and its educational implications;
- experience of working with children with Asperger syndrome across a range of settings;
- the ability to see the world from the child's point of view, and to interpret that view to others;
- the sensitivity to understand the class teacher's perspective, and the factors which may constrain her;
- skills in assessing the child in his particular context;
- the ability to advise on ways of manipulating the classroom environment so that it suits the child's learning style;
- an open-minded positive attitude, and the ability to remain calm;
- skills in delivering INSET;
- knowledge of ways in which the curriculum may effectively be differentiated;

- the ability to foster good relationships with parents, school staff and other professionals, recognising the need for reassurance.

The support teacher may not have all the answers, but will be able to suggest a range of strategies and approaches for the class teacher and support assistant to employ. The development of an atmosphere of mutual trust will be a priority.

The role of the support assistant

The classroom support assistant has a role in relation to the child with Asperger syndrome which differs from the approach to a child with learning difficulties. Very often, children with Asperger syndrome are more comfortable when carrying out learning tasks than when playing. The routine and clear structure of a learning task can be easier to cope with, as long as social interaction with other children is not essential.

Because of the subtle and pervasive nature of the impairment, it is in the ordinariness of moment by moment existence that difficulties may occur for the child with Asperger syndrome. The support assistant, therefore, has to be prepared to operate at an equally subtle and pervasive level, to be present in the fabric of the child's day, to be part of the 'prosthetic' environment, to act as translator, go-between and friend.

Working in close cooperation with the class teacher, school Special Educational Needs Coordinator (SENCO), specialist support teacher (where available), other involved professionals and with parents, the support assistant has to, where possible:

- understand the child's limited ability to interpret social cues;
- interpret situations for the child;
- show the child what is expected of him;
- help in the teaching of appropriate social interaction skills, such as turn-taking;
- guide peers in how to interact with the pupil, engaging their help;
- understand the subtle difficulties of language and communication;
- listen to the child's pattern of language use and be alert to difficulties of interpretation;
- explain, show and make clear to the child when confusion occurs;
- help the child to develop appropriate language use, and to develop awareness;
- understand the sources of rigidity and obsessionality in the child's behaviour;
- anticipate what will cause anxiety, and make changes accordingly;
- analyse and break down situations or activities which are causing alarm;
- make task procedures clearly visible, using visual and pictorial cues;
- support the child in physical activities if clumsiness is a problem;
- assist in making writing tasks easier;
- be prepared for periods of anxiety with appropriate stress-reducing activities;
- regularly evaluate the potential for increasing the child's independence;

- identify gaps in the development of self-help skills in areas such as dressing and washing. Incorporate these into the child's programme;
- identify any organisation difficulties and produce practical and visual aids to help the child;
- support home–school liaison and recording of progress;
- offer appropriate rewarding strategies within individual programmes;
- know when and how to ask for help from teaching and specialist support staff;
- liaise regularly with the class teacher, school SENCO and specialist teaching support staff (if available);
- develop and maintain useful monitoring, evaluating and recording systems.

In addition, the support assistant will need to be:

- calm;
- positive;
- consistent.

and will preferably have a good sense of humour!

Top tips for support assistants

The following is a list of ideas compiled by a group of some 30 support assistants attending a workshop on autism and Asperger syndrome.

They were each asked to recommend five 'Top Tips' derived from their experience of working with children with Asperger syndrome.

Communication
- Simplify your language.
- Give one instruction at a time, not a sequence.
- Keep facial expressions and gestures simple and clear.
- Give the child time to respond.
- Use additional visual clues to help the child understand.
- Be sensitive to the child's attempts to communicate.
- Set up situations which will encourage the child to attempt to communicate.

Social interaction
- Understand that the child may feel threatened by the close proximity of others – especially those his own age.
- Allow for solitariness.
- Go at the child's pace when trying to develop interaction – you may need to 'move down' developmentally.
- Identify what the child likes and dislikes socially – use this knowledge when planning activities.
- The child is more likely to interact with familiar people, so give him time to get to know you, and don't confuse him with many changes of personnel.

Behaviour
- Offer maximum consistency of approach.
- Help the child understand what is expected of him by having clear, predictable routines.
- Introduce any changes gradually.
- Help explain changes by giving visual clues.
- If the child becomes agitated, understand that the usual strategies for calming a child (e.g., trying to sit him on your knee) may have the opposite effect, and wind him up even more.
- If the child has an obsession, don't try to stop it. In time, you may be able to limit it – in the meantime use it positively.

General
- Results and progress can be slow – don't give up! (It often takes a long time to form a relationship.)
- Every child is different – what works for one may not work for another.
- Every child is variable – so if the child is having a 'bad' day, don't feel that it is your fault.
- If all else fails, leave alone. Tomorrow is another day!

Because the long-term aim is for the child with Asperger syndrome to function independently, the best support assistant is the one who does herself out of a job!

Key elements of effective intervention

The key words for intervention are routine, clarity and consistency. Minor environmental changes in the classroom, which simplify the organisation and structure of the room and the tasks, can help the child make sense of expectations.

Useful changes can be made in the following areas of the environment:

- the physical and sensory environment;
- the language and communication environment;
- the social environment;
- the curricular environment.

Specific interventions to enable the child to develop skills and understanding in the areas of Social Interaction, Social Communication and Social Imagination and Play can then be built in. In other words, the approach needs to be remedial as well as compensatory.

Physical and sensory environment

A cluttered, unpredictable, ever-changing environment will only confuse the child with Asperger syndrome and make him anxious. By analysing the child's learning environment, it is possible to devise modifications which will help him.

Organisation and structure

Most classrooms are organised along social lines. The role of social understanding is taken for granted by teachers who may, in fact, not be aware of the role of social understanding within the organisation of their classroom, e.g., in collaborative group work, the sharing of equipment, listening as a group to an instruction. A lot of infant and primary classrooms are organised on group lines, with groups moving around the classroom to access tasks.

It may be necessary to give the child his own 'space' at times during the day. This will be particularly important when a new task is being introduced, since the stress of being part of a group may limit understanding. This 'space' does not need to be a sophisticated individual work station – a desk placed adjacent to the group table, facing away from distractions, can be effective.

It is helpful if the child has a designated seating position within the classroom and keeps the same tray or drawer throughout the year. Where changes need to be made, they must be explained simply and carefully in advance.

Most children adapt happily to the structure of the classroom and are able to make sense of what is happening. However, the child with Asperger syndrome may need an extra layer of structure to help him access the curriculum.

TEACCH

This extra layer of structure is a visual layer. The foundation for this approach can be found within a system developed in North Carolina – Treatment and Education of Autistic and Communication Handicapped Children (TEACCH). The TEACCH system (Schopler *et al.* 1995) recognises that, for children with autism spectrum disorders, the total psychological environment is an important avenue of intervention.

TEACCH was developed in the 1960s by Eric Schopler and Gary Mesibov for use with children with autism. Seen as a 'cradle to grave' approach, it starts with a comprehensive assessment, progresses through structured intervention, and aims to equip students for productive life in the community.

Whereas the TEACCH environment for children with autism is described as *prosthetic*, in respect of Asperger syndrome its use may be better described as *scaffolding*. In the latter case, the degree of environmental modification will be steadily modified over time, rather than being maintained as long-term provision.

The main elements of TEACCH are as follows.

1. Physical structure

This refers to the way in which the environment is organised. There are clear visual boundaries segmenting the space into recognisable parts – to help the children understand what they are expected to do in each area. In the area set aside for 'work', distractions are kept to a minimum.

2. The schedule

This tells the child visually what activities will occur – and in which order. Using objects, photos, pictures, numbers or words (depending on the individual's developmental level), the child is helped to understand a sequence of events.

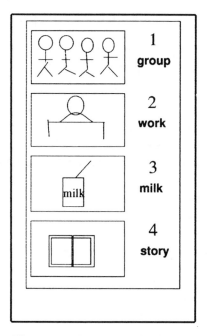

Figure 4.1 Picture schedule

3. Work systems

Through these systems the child is taught:

- How much work will I have to do?
- What work will I have to do?
- When will I have finished?
- What happens when I've finished?

4. Visual clarity

Tasks are presented visually so as to make the expectations clear and highlight the important information.

The following case study is an example of this style of intervention:

- Dean, an eight-year-old boy, was diagnosed at the age of four as having Asperger syndrome. His school career began in an assessment class of 12 pupils attached to a mainstream infant school.
- Dean found the situation very difficult. He would scream and become upset at any changes that took place within the school day.
- Photographs were taken of all the activities likely to be on offer in the class.
- A series of these photographs was stuck on the wall by Dean's table – in the order that activities would happen that day.
- Staff drew Dean's attention to the first photograph, introducing him to his first task.
- On completion of this task, Dean would remove this photo and see what

was to be done next. In this way, Dean began to be able to predict what was to happen next. This enabled him to relax within the situation and access the curriculum.

- Once he was at ease with the photograph timetable, this was replaced by a series of line drawings and words.
- From this, the drawings were replaced with words alone, which, in turn, became a daily list – Dean crossing off each activity as it was completed.
- At this time it was thought that Dean was ready to move into the mainstream infant class on a full-time basis.
- At his review, prior to the move, it was agreed that his Statement should be amended to include help from a Special Support Assistant (SSA) as he moved on.
- The structure continued in the mainstream classroom (a Year 1 class of 28 children with one teacher). Dean's SSA prepared the list each morning and Dean would use it as a way of supporting his understanding of what was happening.
- The list began to be condensed to cover just the main points of the day.
- The list eventually became redundant – without repercussions.
- When Dean moved up to the junior school, his timetable was briefly reintroduced until he had settled – then phased out again.

The visual support offered to Dean appeared to enable him to engage with the activities by giving an extra layer of structure and predictability in his classroom. Other children have adopted personal ways of structuring tasks to help their understanding. One five-year-old boy would use his fingers to list the order of classroom activities. Some others have used a series of comic strip style drawings to guide them through the day. It helps motivate the child if a 'reward' activity is included in the sequence.

The language and communication environment

Children with Asperger syndrome often have good language skills, including extensive vocabularies and the ability to use complex grammatical structures. However, these skills are superficial and mask their difficulties in communication – particularly in the social use of language (pragmatics) and the ability to convey and understand meaning (semantics). These children do not learn the necessary semantic and pragmatic skills from simply being surrounded by a communication-rich environment.

The aim of intervention is to create an environment which will:

- help the child to develop communicative intent, both verbal and non-verbal;
- develop the child's ability to initiate and maintain a conversation;
- enhance the child's understanding of meaning.

Intervention should start at the child's *communication level* – rather than the language level. Although his communication skills may not be developing along the usual lines, he is making a real attempt to enter the communicative process. Our responses to him should reflect this.

Structuring the language environment

It helps if the language environment can be simplified and structured and take account of the following points:

- Address the child by name before giving an instruction, particularly if instructing the class as a group.
- Encourage and reinforce all attempts to communicate.
- Use concrete, direct, explicit instructions – supported by picture prompts where possible.
- If you need to give a sequence of instructions, just give one step at a time.
- Give the child time to respond, then check that he has understood.
- Repeat the instruction if necessary – without rewording it (or the child may think it's a different instruction).
- Teach the child a stock phrase to use when he doesn't understand an instruction – this may prevent frustration on both sides.
- Questions often confuse children with Asperger syndrome. Where possible, turn them into statements. 'The weather today is . . .' rather than 'What's the weather like today?'
- Recognise the child's intentions. They may say, 'Do you want some crisps?' but mean '*I* want some crisps.'
- Guide the child towards the correct response for different situations.
- When looking at text or listening to people speaking, draw the child's attention to the way words are usually put together.
- Try to be aware of the language you use – could it be misinterpreted? Take care not to use sarcasm or irony.
- Offer activities which present opportunities for turn-taking and reciprocity.

Developing the child's skills and understanding

- A key role here is that of *interpreter* – having someone who can help the child to make sense of the world – and help the world understand the child. This may be a support assistant, but classmates can also have a role here.
- If the child echoes words or chunks of language (echolalia), this could mean that he has failed to understand. It may also be an indication of anxiety. Simplify your language and check for stress triggers.
- If the child has particular areas of skill or interest, use these as starting points for language work.
- Help the child to become aware of the needs of the listener, learning how to vary the tone and volume of his voice according to the situation.
- Encourage eye-to-eye contact – without training it.
- The child may understand literal rather than metaphorical or implied meanings. Go through some common metaphors with him, e.g., 'Pull your socks up!' and explain what they mean. Spell out your implied meanings. You may say, 'It's very noisy in here' but you mean 'Be quiet everyone.'

Elizabeth Newson (1992) advises that deliberately teaching a repertoire of metaphors can be productive, and suggests the use of a series of children's booklets by Len Collis, called 'Things We Say: A Book that Helps You Understand What People Mean'. She also indicates the importance of cultivating a verbal sense of humour, using children's illustrated joke books as a starting point, graduating to comic strip books such as *Fungus the Bogeyman*, to encourage an appreciation of irony and satire.

- Help the child to understand the meaning and emotions behind certain facial expressions. Draw his attention to pictures in books and magazines which illustrate different expressions – and to his own face in the mirror.

Role play can be useful for some children in acting out situations involving emotional reactions. Video feedback can help the child to recognise emotions expressed in facial expression, posture and gesture.

The Social Use of Language Programme (SULP, Rinaldi 1992) provides an assessment tool, together with intervention programmes designed to develop social and pragmatic language understanding and use.

For most children, language is a way of entering a stimulating social world. This is not necessarily the case for children with Asperger syndrome.

The social environment

The difficulty in developing fluent interpersonal skills is probably the most noticeable feature of children with Asperger syndrome. These children are not *antisocial*. Rather, they are *asocial* – at times wanting to be part of the social world, but not knowing how to enter it. But children with Asperger syndrome do not pick up social skills incidentally, they need to be specifically taught.

Intervention must start at the child's level of interaction, recognising that he is socially immature – whatever his level of academic performance. It must be borne in mind that the child may be content in solitary pursuits. We should not force the child to join in, but take the approach of enhancing his social skills. The classroom environment should take account of the anxiety that a child can feel by being part of a group. There should be opportunities for the child to have his own 'space' at times.

Other people need to understand the difficulties posed by the child with Asperger syndrome, and the reasons why he behaves the way he does. These children appear to find it easier to relate to adults than to others their own age. This may be because adults make more allowances, and modify their own behaviour towards the child.

The child with Asperger syndrome may appear to be naive and trusting, unable to discriminate between friendly approaches and those approaches which are intended to 'wind them up'. Their peers seem to take on the role of 'buddy' or 'bully'.

Intervention starts with observation, identifying which children are acting positively, and which are potential sources of anxiety. This anxiety may not be immediately obvious. The child may brood on his perception of an incident – reacting negatively at a later date.

Consider the following points when planning intervention:

- Ensure that all staff have an awareness of the social difficulties arising from Asperger syndrome, and are prepared to 'make allowances' in an agreed way.
- With parental agreement, it may be helpful to talk to others in the class/school about Asperger syndrome.
- As part of a general school policy of positive behaviour management, ensure that all children are aware of the unacceptability of bullying.
- Teach the child how to respond to unwanted approaches, since a child who is tormented may become increasingly hostile and aggressive.
- Make sure the child knows which adult to turn to when feeling upset.
- Consider having a quiet area available for the child to retreat to when feeling anxious.
- Analyse the class group and select mature children to act as 'buddies' or a 'circle of friends'.

The 'buddy' system involves identifying another child who is willing to help the child with Asperger syndrome to negotiate difficulties.

When Philip was encouraged to leave the gatepost and come into school, he was given the support of a 'buddy'. This boy helped Philip to get organised for lessons, to follow his timetable and be in the right place at the right time. In return, Philip drew on his own skills to help him with work on the computer. 'Circles of friends' can be built up so that the onus does not fall only on one child.

Developing the child's skills and understanding

1. *The sense of self.* It is often said that children with Asperger syndrome have a high level of egocentricity. This may make it sound as if they choose to act in this way – they don't! They often don't even understand their own feelings and behaviour.

   There may come a time when the child is concerned as to his own well-being. Questions in adolescence from able children such as, 'Am I mad?' cause distress to all concerned.

   The aim of intervention is to increase the child's confidence in himself as an individual, since increased self-esteem reduces anxiety. The following points should be borne in mind:

   - There is a need to strive to give the child a positive image of himself.
   - The time will come when it will be appropriate to tell the child the background to his difficulties. This will need to be discussed by parents and professionals.
   - Once the child is aware of his 'diagnosis', discourage him from blaming Asperger syndrome for everything. Encourage him to think of alternative strategies.
   - The child may need to be taught to develop a 'sense of self'. Encourage him to reflect on his own role in events and activities, using photographs or video and subjective accounts.

Jordan and Powell (1995) explain how this approach is developed.

2. *Interaction with others.* Children with Asperger syndrome lack an awareness of the needs of others in relation to themselves.

Intervention aims to increase the child's desire to interact with others. It may start with increasing the child's awareness of the ways in which other people behave, then work to equip the child to interact with others. To do this it is necessary to teach specific social skills, preferably in realistic, functional settings:

- Identify areas of social interaction where the child particularly struggles. Analyse the skills he needs to improve his performance and teach them in small, achievable steps. For example: how to enter a group; how to talk about things that interest others – not simply 'pet' interests; how to stay involved in the group topic.
- Make the most of activities which lend themselves to working with a partner, e.g., paired reading.
- Give the child the opportunity to play simple board games, e.g., draughts, with a partner. Initially the partner may be a trusted adult, introducing another child to the game later.
- Begin to involve the child in simple team games – in the classroom, in PE or in the playground. Make the child's role in the game very clear.

The curricular environment

The majority of children with Asperger syndrome are educated within mainstream schools. Some teachers feel overwhelmed by the responsibility of teaching such a child within a class group of 30 or more. This is not for any hostile or negative reasons, rather it stems from anxiety about the unknown. They feel they may have to use strategies that are outside the normal repertoire of teaching in order to meet the child's needs. In reality what is needed is a combination of an understanding of Asperger syndrome and good classroom practice.

Teachers need to be informed, tolerant and empathic, in a situation where all staff are aware of the educational implications of Asperger syndrome. Specific impairments are part of Asperger syndrome, but each child will have many strengths which can be developed in school.

In Chapter Three, we considered the educational implications of the impairments of Asperger syndrome, and the psychological theories which inform them. It has been suggested that in Asperger syndrome the child's difficulties stem from impairments of 'Theory of Mind', Central Coherence and Executive Function. Because of this, the child with Asperger syndrome has a different perspective on the world and this is reflected in his learning style. The 'Asperger learning style' is composed of the following characteristics:

The Asperger learning style

41

1. *Motivation.* Competitive motives are absent in the child with Asperger syndrome. He lacks both pride and shame, and has no desire to 'stand out'.

2. *Imitation.* Although he may be able to copy what others do, he finds it hard to adjust these copied movements to his own frame of reference.

3. *Perception.* There is a possibility of inconsistent or unexpected responses to sensory input.

4. *Attention.* The child's focus of attention is often narrow and/or obsessive. Stimulus characteristics may be combined idiosyncratically.

5. *Memory.* The child's memory is likely to be episodic, i.e., events are not stored in the context in which they occurred. Lists of facts may be stored in this way without a meaningful framework to link them.

6. *Sequencing.* The child with Asperger syndrome will have difficulty in following sequences. He may be able to match a sequence but be unable to go beyond the model, to abstract the rule or principle on which it is based. For this reason, changes in sequences of events will distress the child because the overarching principle will not have been recognised.

7. *Problem solving.* The child tries to learn set responses for set situations. He may learn a set of strategies, but not be aware that he possesses them, and therefore be unable to select an appropriate strategy for a new situation.

Accommodating the Asperger syndrome learning style within the National Curriculum

Running through the National Curriculum are common themes which may need to be differentiated to accommodate the particular learning style of the child with Asperger syndrome. To illustrate this, selected elements of the National Curriculum will be viewed from the point of view of a child with Asperger syndrome. Examples of possible difficulty will be outlined, together with suggested intervention strategies.

English: Key Stages 1 and 2

In this example, the young child's difficulties in being able to think flexibly and creatively are impeding his progress in English.

Curriculum area: English	Stages: KS 1 and 2
Examples of difficulties	Suggested strategies
1. Child's ability to think imaginatively is impaired, leading to problems in creative writing.	1. Give the child additional opportunities to write about real things he has experienced. Use this as the basis for developing creative writing. Eg: 'This is what really happened when you went to the seaside, but what would have happened if – it had rained/the car had broken down/you had lost your spending money?' Help the child by talking through the possibilities. Keep creative elements within the child's experience.
2. The child might be quite skilled at reading. He can decode the words, but doesn't fully understand what he's read.	2. Extend the child's understanding by drawing his attention to the illustrations – 'What's happening in the picture?' Ask him to predict what will happen next. Eg: 'What will the boy do now?' Ask him to retell what he's just read. Give preference to books which offer realism rather than fantasy. Give the child ample access to non-fiction books. He will find it easier to retrieve information from these than from stories.

Technology: Key Stages 3 and 4

In this second example, an older student, also limited in his ability to think flexibly, has difficulties with aspects of Technology.

Curriculum area: Technology	Stages: KS 3 and 4
Examples of difficulties	Suggested strategies
1. The student has difficulty with those aspects of Technology which demand a significant level of creative thinking.	1. Choose a project which is practical, relevant to the pupil, and can make use of recent direct experience.
2. The student finds it difficult to choose which materials and equipment to use.	2. Don't overwhelm the student with too many items to choose from. Present no more than 2 alternatives at a time.
3. The student is distracted by irrelevant details. He goes 'off at a tangent' and fails to complete a task.	3. Minimise distractions in the way the materials are set out. Help the student to maintain his focus by offering a written format, with the task outlined in clear steps.
4. The curriculum expects students to have an open-minded approach when developing their ideas, and to explore a range of potential solutions before selecting one. This student may only see one possibility and stick with it rigidly.	4. At first, go along with his single-mindedness, and focus on developing his skills in describing, recording, organising and planning. Later, encourage the consideration of other options and strategies. Structured worksheets may be useful.

Maths: Key Stages 1 and 2

Here are examples of how the child's difficulties with language and communication cause him problems in Maths.

Curriculum area: Mathematics	Stages: KS 1 and 2
Examples of difficulties	Suggested strategies
1. The child has difficulty understanding complex instructions.	1. Simplify your language. Give instructions one step at a time. Use objects and pictures to support the child's understanding.
2. The child is fascinated by numbers and asks the same questions over and over – interrupting the lesson.	2. Set a clear rule. Tell the child he can only ask the same thing perhaps 3 times. Try to set time aside for the child to be able to ask his questions.
3. The child has difficulties understanding the language of Maths. He is particularly confused when different words are used to mean the same thing. Eg: multiply/times.	3. Use practical examples to help the words make sense. Make a collection of words that relate to each concept for the child to refer to.
4. The child isn't sure how to respond to 'Why' questions.	4. Where possible, turn questions into statements with a gap for the child's answer.

Science: Key Stages 3 and 4

In the final example, an older student's progress in Science is impeded by his problems with social interaction.

Curriculum area: Science	Stages: KS 3 and 4
Examples of difficulties	Suggested strategies
1. The student prefers to work alone, and resists having to share a task with another student. Group activities present even more difficulties.	1. Take care in selecting partners and group members. Make the role of each partner/group member clear. Initially, the student may need to have a passive role, perhaps recording results. Gradually equip him to be able to take a more active role.
2. The student fails to show due regard for the safety of himself and others.	2. This area involves imagining the consequences of actions which students with Asperger syndrome will find difficult. It will be important to 'spell out' in the clearest way the possible consequences of different actions. Checking procedures need to be taught and built in as routines.
3. The student is unable to ask for help in lessons.	3. First teach him to recognise that he is 'stuck'. Because he cannot 'put himself in your shoes', he may not realise that you have the information he needs. Specifically teach him how to ask for the help he needs.

Non-curricular areas

For many children with Asperger syndrome, it is not the curriculum that causes them the most difficulty. Rather, it is the non-curricular areas, e.g., assembly, playtime, lunch break, which they find the most challenging and difficult to cope with. It is their behaviour at these times which may first raise their teachers' concerns.

The following are examples of these behaviours:

Ricky, in a reception class, would scream whenever he was asked to sit amongst the other children on the carpet.

At playtime, Bryony would continuously walk around the perimeter of the playground, following the lines of the netball court. She would have nothing to do with the other children.

David spent all his playtime on tiptoe at the edge of the school yard, his eyes fixed on the Town Hall clock.

In assembly, Simon showed no awareness of the other 200 children. He saw no reason why he couldn't talk one-to-one with the head teacher.

Teachers may feel that their chief role is to teach the curriculum, and feel less secure in their ability to develop a child's interpersonal skills – particularly to the extent required for a child with Asperger syndrome. The following information aims to give starting points for intervention by offering examples of good practice in a variety of situations.

Assembly

Assembly can be a difficult time. There is hustle and bustle on the way into the hall, and on the way back. Lots of children are sitting closely together. The rules seem different to those which operate in the classroom, and are difficult for a child with Asperger syndrome to understand. An adult stands at the front asking rhetorical questions, and sometimes shouting.

Strategies to help the child with Asperger syndrome cope with assembly include:

- First, consider whether going into assembly is a priority for the child – particularly if he is very anxious. Initially, the time may be better spent in a quiet one-to-one activity, focusing on other targets.
- When the child is generally more relaxed, he can gradually be brought into assembly.
- Clearly explain the rules which apply in assembly, using visual prompts to reinforce them.
- Allow the child to sit at the edge of a group, rather than in the middle. Make sure he has sufficient personal space to feel comfortable.
- Praise the child for sitting quietly.
- Encourage another child to take on a 'buddy' role, prompting and offering guidance.

Playtime

For the majority of children, playtime is the best part of the school day but children with Asperger syndrome may dread playtime. Playtime is unstructured. Children are noisy and boisterous. There are no rules.

Social pairings and groups develop.

Teachers often report that the child with Asperger syndrome has no friends and is a loner in the playground.

Playtime presents opportunities for developing the child's social skills – whilst accepting his need to relax in his own way.

Strategies to help the child with Asperger syndrome cope with playtime include:

- Setting a playground 'ethos' in which collaboration is encouraged.
- Accepting that the child with Asperger syndrome may *need* to be on his own at playtime – as respite from the social demands of the classroom.
- Organising simple, structured, social games – where each individual's role is obvious. Prompt the child to join in.
- Encouraging the child to observe the activities taking place in the playground. Talk them through. Find one activity which appeals to the child and, with peer support, encourage him to join in.
- Teaching the child useful 'opening lines' which will help him to initiate a conversation. Children with Asperger syndrome often want to be a part of things – but they don't know how. James, for instance, would carry a football programme in his pocket, and approach other boys, asking if they wanted to look at it with him.

Moving around school

In the primary school there is movement, and the potential for confusion, at certain key times of day. This increases enormously at secondary school when there is often wholesale movement at the end of each lesson.

These times can be stressful for the child with Asperger syndrome, simply because of the sheer volume of children moving through a small area. Additional anxiety is generated in the secondary school by the need to find the right room in a huge building.

Strategies to help the child with Asperger syndrome cope with moving around the school include:

- Initially staggering the child's arrival/departure so that the volume of 'traffic' is less overwhelming.
- Arranging visits to the secondary school prior to transfer, to give the child the opportunity to learn its layout.
- Establishing a network of 'buddies' or a 'circle of friends' who will be available to act as 'guides'.

In the dining room

Dining rooms can be noisy and very socially demanding. Children are expected to eat publicly alongside six or eight other children. Most school lunch times involve queueing – an activity which many children with Asperger syndrome find difficult to tolerate.

Strategies to help the child with Asperger syndrome cope with the school dining room include:

- Establishing clear rules, reinforced by visual prompts.
- Role play lunchtime routines in a quiet, empty dining room.
- Consider allowing the child to be at the front or the end of the queue – rather than in the middle of everyone. This will feel less threatening to the child.
- Alert lunchtime supervisors to the child's difficulties and the strategies which are being used.
- Teach simple conversation skills to help him join in with the others on his table.

Asking for help and solving problems

'Miss! How do you do this?' Most children readily ask for help when they are unsure. Children with Asperger syndrome find this particularly difficult to do – for a combination of reasons:

- Children with Asperger syndrome have difficulty with problem solving – in combining the elements of a task to help guide them towards a solution. Asking for someone's help is one element in the problem-solving process. They don't necessarily see the link between the problem and outside help.
- Because children with Asperger syndrome are impaired in their ability to recognise that others have different points of view, they may not realise that someone else *has* a solution to their problem.

Unfortunately, this behaviour can be misinterpreted as laziness or lack of motivation – thinking the child is avoiding work, rather than unable to get on with it.

Strategies to help the child with Asperger syndrome ask for the help he needs include:

- Having an awareness of which tasks cause the child particular difficulty.
- If the child is having difficulty in interpreting a task, try to work alongside him. Do the task yourself and draw his attention to what you are doing. Let him have a turn at doing part of the task. Gradually reduce your input until the child can work independently.
- When a child has completed a task, get him to reflect on his own learning, talking through what he did and how he did it.
- Specifically, teach the child how to recognise when he is 'stuck', and how to ask for help.

Working with others

Teachers expect children to be in close proximity to others at several times during the school day. They may be unaware of the stress this may cause the child with Asperger syndrome who has such difficulty in relating to others.

The child with Asperger syndrome has little or no awareness of others' feelings or of the impact of his own behaviour on others. They may passively accept the presence of other children, but some children become tense just because someone is sitting too near them. Contact will be one-sided – from the other child to them, but rarely reciprocated.

Increasingly, children in school are expected to work collaboratively with a partner or a small group. With careful planning and preparation, the child with Asperger syndrome can be included in these activities.

Strategies to help the child with Asperger syndrome to work with others include:

- Having an awareness of the level of social contact that the child can tolerate without becoming anxious.
- Initially allowing the child to sit on the edge of a group activity, perhaps with a support assistant between him and the other children.
- Considering seating arrangements. The child may feel more comfortable if the next child sits diagonally across from him – rather than beside him.
- Once the child will tolerate sitting near others, the support assistant can set up simple turn-taking tasks – at first just with her; later involving another child; finally the support assistant 'backs off', encouraging the child to work with his partner.
- There may be opportunities to use the child's own special skills or interests, perhaps getting him to show a partner how to do something on the computer.
- Clearly defining and teaching each person's role in a group task or team activity – removing uncertainty for the child with Asperger syndrome.

School life becomes easier for children with Asperger syndrome when the adults around them recognise the extent to which social demands result in stress. Intervention and support in this area pays dividends in terms of academic attainments since stress impedes learning.

Summary

- Start from the child's level.
- Attempt to see the world from the child's point of view.
- Adapt the school environment to facilitate the child's learning.
- Consult and collaborate – with parents as well as professionals.
- Consider specific interventions to develop the child's skills in Social Interaction, Social Communication and Flexible Thinking.
- Become familiar with the underlying psychological explanations of the child's learning style.

Chapter 5

Behavioural Intervention

The core difficulties of Asperger syndrome are exactly those which could be expected to lead to behavioural difficulties for a child.

The notion proposed by the TEACCH system – that people with autism operate from within a different 'culture' – is illuminating. In this sense, children with autism do not 'speak our language', do not understand our ways of communicating, and may need an 'interpreter'. They may be seen as having extreme difficulty at times in 'cracking the code' of our way of being.

Specific areas of difficulty which impact on behaviour are:

The core difficulties and implications for behaviour

Decoding people

Simon Baron-Cohen (1996) describes 'mind-reading' as a game of social chess, involving constantly changing strategies in the negotiation of 'social plot and counter plot'. He goes on to point out that the way we play this social chess is intuitive; it does not, typically, involve laborious logical reasoning. In contrast, for the child with Asperger syndrome, interpreting the behaviour of others is difficult, even at the simplest level.

When Patrick, looking at an illustration of a crying child, was asked to talk about the picture, he named the tears 'drips of water' – totally missing the emotional point.

So, in the classroom situation, the significance of the stern look, the raised eyebrow and other subtle, non-verbal means of classroom management are lost on the child with Asperger syndrome.

The young child with Asperger syndrome simply cannot see himself as a member of a group and may turn his back on the teacher at story time, or trample over another child to get to what he wants. But there is no intention to ignore or hurt others. The frustrated class teacher, seeking advice on such a child, will often refer to 'extreme non-compliance'.

Encoding self

Through understanding others we understand ourselves and vice versa. The child with Asperger syndrome misses out on the creation of an inner life as well as a social life.

A simple request to one child to 'give me a smile' was met by him putting his fingers to the corners of his mouth, lifting them up. Another child found it hard to understand what made him upset and why he cried. He used to try to push his tears back in. He felt out of control, and this only added to his distress.

For Jordan and Powell (1995), the child with such extreme difficulties in understanding and interpreting emotion is unable to give meaning to his own participation in events in his life, lacking a sense of 'experiencing self'.

Imagination

Imagination gives us the ability to pose alternatives in the mind, that is, alternative images or interpretations of our own behaviour and the behaviour of others and also to plan alternative courses of action.

Alex was a six-year-old boy who usually ignored other children in the playground. For two consecutive days, a little girl had included him in her game – much to the delight of his support assistant. On the third day, when the same friendly girl asked him to play, he brusquely replied, 'No! Go away', neither anticipating the effect this would have on her, nor registering her response when it occurred.

Cracking the language code

Instructions given to the whole class are frequently not noticed by the child with Asperger syndrome, who doesn't recognise they apply to him too. Conversely, if the child with Asperger syndrome is sitting amongst his classmates while the teacher talks to them all, he will very often shout out responses as if the teacher was just talking to him. This behaviour is not deliberately disruptive, but it may appear to be.

As the children sat quietly at their tables in the nursery, waiting for the teacher to begin reading a poem, Callum called out, 'I'm not staying for lunch today, I'm having lunch with Mummy.' 'Yes, that's right', the teacher replied, and again tried to begin to read the poem. Callum interrupted again, 'I'm not staying for lunch today, I'm having lunch with Mummy.' The teacher acknowledged his comment, and again began to read. Callum's deep monotone again boomed out, 'I'm not staying . . .'

'Now, I'd like you to do your exercises', said the teacher, half way through the English lesson. Bryn got down on the floor and started to perform physical jerks. He was not trying to be funny.

Peter was playing a game where the children were asked to be a particular number. He began to cry, 'I don't want to be a number, I'm not a number.'

Rigidity and rule-bound behaviour

This may arise from the inability to abstract and infer simple social rules from the problems with central coherence described earlier. It can lead to episodes of confrontation.

Alex did not see why he should work through endless similar Maths examples – he had done one, and he knew how to do the others. Doing more of the same seemed pointless to him.

Exclusive interests and obsessions

Certain behaviours or interests appear to 'take over' at times at the expense of learning, social interaction or other activities. But the 'reason' for stopping or postponing such behaviours is usually ours, not the child's. For the child, they are intrinsically rewarding, and it can be difficult to find a competing reward.

Compulsivity, perseveration, perfectionism

These features can lead to the child not being able to stop an activity or conversely, not being able to start. This can be seen as uncooperative behaviour.

Imran would write a word, but become frustrated because it was not as perfect as the printed word in his book. He would rub it out and rewrite it over and over agin. He was never satisfied with what he produced, and never completed a page of work.

Integrated learning

Minutiae are attended to, and concrete detail required, but generalisation does not occur. Concepts are not derived from facts. The child may excel in one aspect of a subject, but be unable to tackle other aspects.

Clyde, aged nine, could multiply and divide four-digit numbers. He was given a Maths test in which the calculations were presented as problems to solve. He wept bitterly, unable to understand what to do, saying, 'You didn't teach me these. I can't do them.'

Sensory experience

In autism, hypersensitivity or hyposensitivity may occur visually and aurally, sometimes with the additional involvement of taste, smell and touch. This can lead to extreme reactions, modulating difficulties and overreactions to relatively subtle changes. Though less marked and much less frequent in Asperger syndrome, children can be extra sensitive in this way.

Motor control

There may be poor coordination, and difficulty with handwriting. This can make a child vulnerable to teasing in the playground and PE, and it may lead to the avoidance of writing tasks in the classroom.

Russell refused to write. His support assistant arranged for him to use the computer instead and he went on to experiment with a variety of writing styles.

Approaches to managing behaviour in Asperger syndrome

Asperger syndrome: *'quintessentially a disorder of human relationships'*.
(Tantam 1987)

Behaviour difficulties occur in the social arena – which is exactly the area in which people with Asperger syndrome experience most problems. The rules of social behaviour are invented, often subtle, changed by negotiation and unwritten. Although we teach the skill of reading step by step, we expect children to acquire the skills of social interaction without explicit teaching. Children with Asperger syndrome find this very difficult.

All behaviour serves a purpose: it is functional, or at least it is intended to be. In order to analyse the functions of any particular behaviour, we need to put aside moral perspective or pet beliefs, and refrain from imposing intuitive or subjective interpretations on the behaviour of others.

In order to intervene in an attempt to change the behaviour of children with Asperger syndrome, it is first necessary to understand the function or purpose of the behaviour – *from the point of view of the child*. It is important to look at the behaviour and the events surrounding it, as if through an 'Asperger lens'.

Simple observation, recording and behavioural intervention are not enough, since the 'trigger' to behaviour may be almost undetectable and the function the behaviour is serving may be quite unexpected from our point of view.

Ryan, aged five, suddenly began banging on the living room wall while his parents were talking to the specialist teacher. The conversation paused, Ryan's parents looking bewildered at this sudden inexplicable loud banging. The teacher noticed a faint sound of banging coming from the house next door. Alert to the frequent sensory hypersensitivity of children within the autism spectrum, she was able to 'tune in' to the world from Ryan's point of view – and to understand the 'trigger' to his behaviour.

Before 'reading' the behaviour of the child with Asperger syndrome, it helps to widen the field of our perception. We need to check which 'lens' we are using and pose likely possibilities from the point of view of the Asperger lens on the world. Use of the 'Asperger lens' in appraising behavioural difficulties occurring in children with Asperger syndrome helps to locate the source of the difficulty and to determine appropriate and, therefore, effective intervention.

The case studies which follow demonstrate how this applies.

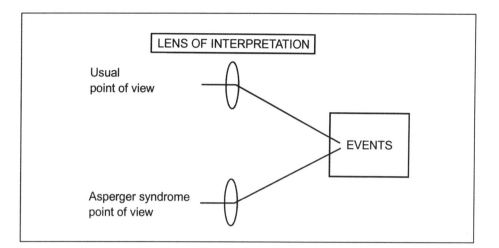

Figure 5.1 The Asperger lens of interpretation

Case study 1

SAM: Sam continuously rolls a pencil rapidly and noisily between his hands – distracting the other children in his primary class.

Theory: To use the child's obsession as a reward, rather than trying to eliminate it.

Original Had the aim of eliminating the pencil-rolling behaviour.
intervention: Rewards were offered, but were ineffective.

But:

What would the Asperger lens show us?
- Pencil-rolling behaviour is 'obsessional'
- To some extent it is necessary.

New intervention
- Use pencil-rolling behaviour as a reward.
- Sam is allowed to roll his pencil during 'transition' times, when children are moving about and the classroom is noisier.

Case study 2

PHILIP: It is 9 a.m. Philip is wrapped round the gatepost at his secondary school entrance. He says he 'can't walk'.

Theory: Develop alternative skills.
Build self-esteem.

Remove the source of difficulty.
Reduce stress.
Re-establish cooperation.

**Original
intervention:** Fellow pupils try to pull Philip off the gatepost
and drag him into school.
Teachers quiz him about where the 'pain' is.

But:

> **What would the Asperger lens show us?**
> - Philip experiences motor difficulties.
> - He is not good at PE and the teacher is not empathic.
> - Today the first lesson is PE.
>
> **New intervention**
> - Liaison and planning with senior staff.
> - In the short term, providing an alternative to PE, while re-establishing school attendance and reducing stress.
> - Giving Philip the opportunity to teach a less able pupil computer skills – raising his self-esteem and confidence.
> - Offering staff (including the PE teacher) in-service training.

Case study 3

CONNOR: Whenever Connor sees a baby, he hits it. This causes
particular problems at the end of the school day, when
many of the mums are waiting with babies in pushchairs.

Theory: Use of rules and structured environment.
Direct teaching of empathy.

**Original
intervention:** A behavioural support teacher attempts to
counsel Connor.
They make a scrapbook about babies and the teacher
explains how vulnerable they are.
He tries to get Connor to reflect on what he was like as a
baby.
He becomes *more* obsessed with hitting babies.

But: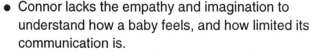

> **What would the Asperger lens show us?**
> - Connor lacks the empathy and imagination to understand how a baby feels, and how limited its communication is.
> - He is angered by babies' crying, and is possibly hypersensitive to loud, unexpected sound.

> **New intervention**
> - Connor is given the rule: 'No hitting babies.'
> - He leaves school by a different door – no longer confronted by a row of prams.
> - Work on developing empathy is carried out:
>   - (a) in school, by his support assistant – e.g., he is taught not to laugh if someone falls over in the playground, but to ask if they are alright;
>   - (b) at home – he is rewarded for not shouting if his grandma coughs, having been given a clear rule.

Case study 4

OLIVER: Prompted by fellow pupils, and to their great amusement, 13-year-old Oliver was producing 'smutty' notes on a school computer, and handing round copies. He quoted some of the overtly sexual statements to female members of staff.

Theory: Identify gaps in knowledge and skills and structure the environment.

Original intervention: Staff express shock and consternation.
Warning of exclusion if behaviour continues.
A set of behavioural targets and a recording system are introduced.

But:

> **What would the Asperger lens show us?**
> - Oliver is naive about sexual matters.
> - He is anxious to have friends and is pleased that the other boys are laughing.
> - He doesn't realise that the boys are laughing *at* him – he thinks they are now his friends.
>
> **New intervention**
> - The material is taken off the word processor.
> - Explanations are given about acceptable language and behaviour in sexual matters.
> - Oliver's social unease is recognised.
> - His wish to have friends is addressed.
> - Oliver's mum is involved in discussions about the need to talk to him about the nature and implications of Asperger syndrome.
> - A modified behavioural plan is introduced, focusing on just two achievable targets:
>   - (a) completing classwork to the teacher's satisfaction;
>   - (b) bringing the correct equipment to the lesson.

Case study 5

ADAM: Aged six years, Adam is noisy and uncooperative.
He has 'deliberately' broken the computer.

Theory: Stress reduction.
Structured environment.

Original intervention: Teacher rebukes Adam, frequently raising her voice to him in the classroom.

But:

What would the Asperger lens show us?
- Adam is in a very cramped and crowded classroom, with a desk next to the musical instrument shelf – he turns round and uses them to make a noise.
- Adam has a loud, monotone voice with which he calls out in class. He is unaware of the disruptive effect this has on others.
- He is unnerved by his teacher's frequently raised voice.
- As his stress level rises, he becomes more noisy, less cooperative and less controlled in his behaviour.

New intervention
- The TEACCH principles for organising the classroom environment are explained to his teacher.
- The musical instruments are placed elsewhere.
- Instead of shouting at Adam across the classroom, his teacher is encouraged to give him instructions and information via the support assistant – his 'interpreter'.
- The teacher is offered in-service training, and given an information pack on Asperger syndrome.

Case study 6

JEFF: This secondary school boy is described as 'dangerous'. He's brought a screwdriver into school and intends to use it against boys who, he believes, are teasing and bullying him.

Theory: Recognise the lack of subtlety in his social interaction. Understand his vulnerability to teasing and bullying, and intervene to prevent it.

Original intervention: Staff threaten exclusion and, after investigation, find no evidence of bullying.

But: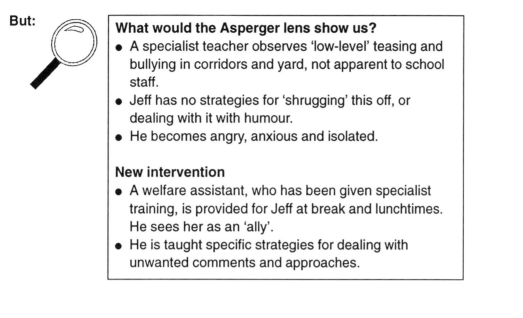

> **What would the Asperger lens show us?**
> - A specialist teacher observes 'low-level' teasing and bullying in corridors and yard, not apparent to school staff.
> - Jeff has no strategies for 'shrugging' this off, or dealing with it with humour.
> - He becomes angry, anxious and isolated.
>
> **New intervention**
> - A welfare assistant, who has been given specialist training, is provided for Jeff at break and lunchtimes. He sees her as an 'ally'.
> - He is taught specific strategies for dealing with unwanted comments and approaches.

Case study 7

REBECCA: This young girl makes inappropriate remarks to family visitors, e.g., saying, 'When are you going?' just as people arrive.

Theory: Provide alternative responses.

Original intervention: Parents are angry. They rebuke and criticise her.

But:

> **What would the Asperger lens show us?**
> - Rebecca has an obsession with 'time'.
> - She is unaware that her comments seem impolite.
>
> **New intervention**
> - Parents learn to remain calm.
> - They teach her more appropriate and acceptable things to do and say, e.g., 'How long can you stay?'

The main points of the behavioural interventions include:

- To identify behaviour is not to specify need.
- All behaviours reflect interactions between events on the outside, and the world within the person – as much for the 'observer' as for the 'observed'.
- Personal interpretations of events are central to feelings experienced and motivations to behave.
- There is a requirement for observation, an open mind and empathy, along with the ability to understand and read behaviour.
- An understanding of the Asperger view of the world is essential.

Summary

Preventing behavioural difficulty

In Asperger syndrome, *'most of the stress comes from living in a society where everyone is expected to conform to a set pattern.'*

Lynda Bannister (Mother of John)

Given the nature of their social difficulties, everyday life must be a source of great difficulty, anger and incomprehension for children with autism spectrum disorders. They are particularly prone to stress.

Donna Williams (1996), a person with Asperger syndrome, writes, 'People who are in a constant state of stress and discomfort also develop strategies to help calm themselves. For some people, this might be rocking or humming or tapping themselves. For others, this might be carrying something around with them.' She links this constant stress to sensory hypersensitivity and the effects of environmental overload in her own case.

Levels of stress

Writing about her ten-year-old son with Asperger syndrome, Lynda Bannister describes three levels of stress:

At level 1, he is relatively calm and happy, eating and sleeping well, able to cope with minor irritations, reasonably sociable and giving good eye contact. In fact, a visitor to the home would be hard-pressed to tell which of the children had autism.

At level 2 though, he is 'edgy, fidgety, irritable, displaying mild symptoms of autism'. He does not sleep well, does not sit to eat a full meal, he talks to himself and does detailed drawings involving maps, games, boxes and numbers. A small annoyance may produce a tantrum. Eye contact is fleeting. Whereas at level 1, John hates swearing and tells other children off if they swear, at level 2 he swears himself and giggles about it.

At level 3, Lynda Bannister describes her son as 'full blown autistic'. Violent and aggressive, he shouts and swears badly, is hyperactive and can't sleep. He won't eat, wets his bed and develops phobias. Shrugging off company of any sort, he giggles hysterically – then cries bitterly. 'He draws, draws, draws, pages and pages of very detailed pictures, the higher his stress level, the more intricate the picture and the harder the picture is to understand. It is like a computer that has gone into overdrive, spilling out pages and pages of garble – "does not compute, does not compute".'

Lynda Bannister attributes this stress to her son being forced to do something which makes no sense to him – a situation in which children with Asperger syndrome often find themselves. At home the family adapts to John as an individual, not expecting him to do things he cannot do – regardless of what might be appropriate at his age. Anticipation of a difficult situation will also cause stress, as will tiredness and lack of exercise. Finally, when he is under stress, John is unable to learn socially at the same time as academically. Gaps in learning themselves cause further difficulties and lead to further stress.

Mrs Bannister's advice to her son's teacher was, 'Take the pressure out of the situation and let him be himself, all muddled up . . . Forget trying to teach him anything until he is calm enough to receive it – or you are wasting your time . . . Let him show you how and where he really is. Listen to him, let *him* lead the way, remove any pressure . . . to prevent him creating havoc for himself and others.'

Stress reduction

Specialist schools for children with autism recognise the need to identify stress and take steps to avoid or reduce it. The Lodden school, for example, recognised the need to capitalise on the times of day when the children were likely to be both calm and alert. At these times, challenging learning activities are offered. Conversely, when the children are at their most anxious, stress-reducing activities are offered. Interestingly, the Lodden staff discovered that the children were more likely to be stressed in the earlier part of the day, and therefore start the day with the least-demanding activities. Gradually, as the day progresses, the level of challenge is increased, with stress-reducing approaches introduced again as the day draws to a close. This is in direct contrast to the approach often taken in primary schools, and in schools and centres for children with behavioural difficulties where the morning is often extended to give early application to study, and more relaxed and rewarding activities begin after lunch.

Lynda Bannister refers to her son's need at times to get outside and run around. Again, in specialist schools for children with autism, emphasis is often placed on the use of vigorous physical activity. At the Higashi school in Boston, physical activity features strongly throughout the day, indoors and outdoors, even including group jogging from home-base to school.

In her autobiography, Temple Grandin (Grandin and Scariano 1986) writes, 'Doing physical labour eased my nerve attacks.'

In Great Britain, Storm House School, run by the National Autistic Society, has developed an extensive programme of outdoor pursuits with their students (Evans 1997).

Donna Williams (1996) points to the influence of fatigue on stress, noting that, '*REAL* breaks of between five minutes to an hour in between participation can help people to sustain personal stress or information overload caused by participation. Breaks should be a peaceful and relaxing time with no non-calming and non-welcomed stimulation.' Other approaches she recommends include a lessening or absence of *unnecessary* stimulation, no unnecessary touching, and the provision of gentle, quiet, steady, calming sounds.

The judicious use of stress-releasing activities within the mainstream setting can help prevent behavioural disturbance.

Ashley's teachers were worried at how he would cope with the school building extension since he is easily distracted and unnerved by noise. The support teacher suggested that for part of the school day during this period of disruption, Ashley should be taken out of school by his Special Support Assistant. She was to work on a programme of independence skills, social interaction and practical Maths – through trips to local shops. This served to reduce Ashley's stress, while providing useful learning experiences. The building period passed without incident.

Stress, if left unrecognised, can lead to escalation in anxiety and obsessions, leading to an increase in aggressive or withdrawn behaviour with a possible onset of depression or psychiatric disorder.

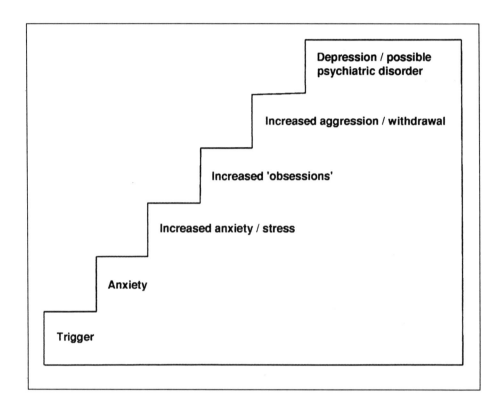

Figure 5.2 Steps in the escalation of stress in Asperger syndrome

A general review of the stress level of the child with Asperger syndrome is always useful if behavioural difficulties are being experienced. Steps may then be taken to improve the underlying conditions which may be causing stress and also to offer opportunities for de-stressing through relaxation or physical exercise within the context of the mainstream environment.

Structuring the environment for prevention

A key feature of the success of the TEACCH approach to the education of children with autism is the recognition of the core difficulty of *rigidity* in autism. That is, that children with autism need to *control* their environment and to adhere to rules and routines. For the children themselves, the experience may be one of *being controlled*, as a young university student with Asperger syndrome (Peers 1997) eloquently describes it, 'Build obsessions into goals, use obsessions in a positive way without letting them rule your life. BE IN CONTROL!!!!'

The need to control can, however, lead to a battle of wills – the teacher's need to direct versus the child's need to control.

The TEACCH system offers a way of *sharing control*, so that issues are externalised. Here is an explicit visual and physical structure which can be 'read' by the child so that daily life in school becomes predictable. The importance of organising the environment to compensate for the child's difficulties is outlined in Chapter Four, together with ways of adapting the environment at several levels. These methods should lead to a reduction in conflict situations and should serve to reduce stress in the pupil with Asperger syndrome.

Use of rules

Because children with Asperger syndrome are often rule-bound and driven by routine, rules can be used positively to prevent behavioural difficulties.

A class teacher using the 'Rules, Praise and Ignore' approach (Madsen *et al.* 1968) will make life easier for the child with Asperger syndrome. However, the principle of explaining the rules of the situation can be extended. Activities where a teacher would assume the rules were known may need to be 'unpacked'. For example, the rules for 'lining up' or for 'going out to play'. Some of these are addressed in the non-curricular section of Chapter Four.

At a more subtle level, the child may need to be involved in discussion of the rules for 'getting someone's attention' or 'how the teacher gets the children's attention'. Sometimes the child with Asperger syndrome will apply the rules universally himself, telling the teacher when a child is breaking a rule, or, inappropriately, telling a burly smoker on a bus that smoking is not allowed. The usefulness of rules in preventing behaviour problems is that they are 'neutral', allowing for an appeal to an objective standard and reducing the need for confrontation.

A non-confrontational, objective and emotionally detached approach

A battle of wills with a child with Asperger syndrome is always to be avoided, since it cannot be won. The lack of negotiating skills, imagination and empathy in the child with Asperger syndrome can be evidenced as an apparent 'extreme stubbornness'. Cajoling, threatening and shows of emotion may lead to an increase in stress in the child, but not to cooperation. Calm, orderly and emotionally neutral approaches to negotiation with the child have the best chance of working.

Preparation and rehearsal

An advantage of the TEACCH approach is the degree of predictability it gives to the child's day with its use of sequenced, pictorial, diagrammatic or even written timetables. The system also allows for visible alteration of a sequence of events so that the child is not suddenly exposed to unexpected change. Sudden change produces anxiety and stress and can trigger behavioural difficulties. Wherever a change which is likely to cause any degree of anxiety can be anticipated, it is advisable to prepare the child beforehand. Role-play, cartoon conversation strips, or prompt cards can be useful aids to this process.

Allowing for interests and obsessions

Very often, the 'obsessions' or 'circumscribed interests' which are found in children with Asperger syndrome serve as hobbies, giving positive pleasure to the child. Rather than attempting to remove these completely, it is helpful to allow the child his 'hobby' under clearly recognised conditions, e.g.:

- *Identified time*: at breaks, playtimes, lunchtime, during transitions, or when given a 'bus ticket' or coloured band.
- *Identified place*: on the carpet, in the story corner, or when in the playground.
- *Identified number*: same question no more than three times, or the special subject for five minutes then change topic.

Some 'obsessions' may need to be eliminated, others not.

On arriving home from school, Matthew liked (needed ?) to get a clean sheet of paper and begin to write a sequence of numbers: 1, 2, 3, 4, 5, 6 . . . and so on. He would continue well into the thousands, once reaching 42,000! A concerned teacher tried to eliminate this behaviour – a course of action which caused Matthew to become increasingly distressed, both at home and at school. His number writing had actually been serving to release tension at the end of the school day – and it did no one any harm. He was subsequently allowed to continue writing numbers, and his stress reduced again.

On the other hand, Steven liked to take hold of and bury his face in the long hair of some of the little girls in his class – a clearly unacceptable behaviour. The girls themselves carried out the programme which extinguished the behaviour by saying firmly, 'I don't like that' as they took his hands and removed them from their hair.

As Howlin and Rutter (1987) noted, obsessional activities can also be very useful:

As reinforcers or rewards

Joshua, in the nursery, was provided with an 'object schedule', each item being pinned in sequence to the back of a cupboard – to illustrate the order of his morning. Thomas the Tank Engine was last in the sequence. If 'Thomas' and the railway track had been brought out earlier, no other activities would have been possible.

As an inroad to more acceptable behaviours
Malcolm spends hours drawing diagrams of routes, roads and motorways. His mother started to encourage him to fill in other details, developing maps with him. This is now being used as a possible entry into fiction also with Tolkien's stories and the Narnia stories.

To facilitate social interaction
Max has been very solitary in his mainstream nursery and early year classes. Now he has more spoken language and can take turns. When he plays with the trainset on the classroom playmat other children are accepted and he has recently been involved in some joint play with the other boys, sharing the trains.

'Prevention is better than cure' – an old adage applicable in the context of Asperger syndrome.

- Structure the environment for prevention.
- Prepare for change, and use rehearsal before the real event where possible.
- Use rules positively.
- Adopt calm, objective, emotionally neutral approaches to negotiation.
- Allow for interests and obsessions, and incorporate these into plans and programmes.
- Be alert to the possibility of stress, and take steps to reduce it by removing potential stress triggers.

Summary

One of the major obstacles to solving 'behaviour problems' can be impulsive responding on the part of the adult. A difficult situation can be made more problematic by inadvertent reinforcement of the problem behaviour.

Four-year-old Joshua refused to come to the table to draw. The nursery nurse insisted. He ran away screaming. Allowed to take his time, and encouraged to come by another child, he eventually came to the table – but refused to pick up a pencil. The nursery nurse insisted. A screaming tantrum ensued. A pattern of behaviour was set up. Soon, pencil and paper, writing or drawing tasks acted as a cue for Joshua to start screaming.

Specific intervention in behavioural difficulties

Make a plan

In order to avoid setting up a worse 'secondary' behaviour problem through inappropriate responses to the initial difficulty, it helps to step back and make a plan.

Step 1: Enlist support
Two heads are often better than one, and 'airing' the problem with someone (the SENCO, a visiting support teacher, the educational psychologist, a parent) will often bring to light new aspects of the situation and a better plan may emerge.

Step 2: Look for the positives
Very often, when a child is presenting difficult behaviour, this begins to dominate our thinking, and we can lose sight of his strengths, abilities and progress in other areas. A spiral of anxiety, anger and concern may develop and lead to a distorted perception of the problem. This will only make intervention more difficult.

As soon as a 'problem behaviour' begins to preoccupy the teaching focus, it is important to counteract negativity and identify possible reinforcers by building a profile of the child's strengths, interests, skills and preferred activities.

Step 3: Identify the purpose or function of the behaviour of the child
All behaviour is functional. Its purpose is to produce a result. 'My fixations reduced arousal and calmed me' (Grandin and Scariano 1986).

It is not always possible to identify the function a behaviour has for the person with Asperger syndrome. Careful 'detective work' by the teacher using the 'Asperger lens' can bring forward some useful hypotheses.

Step 4: Define the exact nature of the problem
It is useful to define the problem clearly in behavioural terms. The terms 'aggression' or 'tantrums' do not make it clear what the child actually does. Specify the actual behaviours.

Step 5: Observe and record
A useful observation tool is the STAR chart (Zarkowska and Clements 1988). This observation approach focuses attention not just on the child's behaviour, but on all the surrounding events and actions. In this way, the *setting conditions* are outlined, *triggers* for the behaviours are noted, the child's *actions* and those of others are detailed, and the *results* are reported.

Careful analysis of the resulting data will then often indicate a pattern of events, and highlight useful starting points for intervention at the following levels:

Setting conditions: For Philip, wrapped round the school gatepost, the anticipation of having PE first lesson provided the setting which had triggered the behaviour. It also suggested the intervention approach.

Triggers: Jeff's anger was triggered by teasing, cruel remarks and gestures which were imperceptible to his subject teachers.

Actions: Sam's pencil-rolling served to reduce stress and was part of his obsessional activity.

Results: Oliver was given 'friendly' attention by the boys in his group when he printed sexually explicit material on the computer.

Design the programme

Careful observation against a background of understanding Asperger syndrome is the key to effective intervention in behavioural problems.

Facilitating alternative behaviour

As with any behavioural intervention programme, a positive approach is more effective in producing longer-term change than attempts to eliminate or extinguish behaviours. This is where the list of the child's strengths, interests, skills and preferred activities comes into play. Very often, 'obsessional' interests then may be used as reinforcers, as with Joshua in the nursery in the example given above.

Relating the rewards to the child

Again, the notes outlining the child's positive attributes will help in the selection of the most powerful rewards to be incorporated in the behaviour programme.

Max was given a coloured counter for cooperating on tasks, he could then exchange these in his TEACCH corner for sweets.

Back-up rewards from home can be very powerful. As a reward, Malcolm is taken out to explore new routes.

However, positive intervention should *remain* positive! Sebastian was given a home-school diary in which both ticks and crosses were recorded – achievements *and* misdemeanours. Sensitive to imperfection and failure, Sebastian would say to his support assistant, 'This is awful. I suppose you will be writing it down in the book, will you?' After a particularly difficult day, his mother burst into tears at the sight of all the crosses on the page. Exit Sebastian with the diary – which was never seen again!

Rewards must be powerful, meaningful, consistent and predictable at the outset of any behavioural programmes in order to be effective.

Using graded change techniques

Change is difficult to cope with, particularly so for children with Asperger syndrome because of the core rigidity. Change is best introduced very gradually indeed.

Simon screamed when taken into assembly. The support assistant initially sat with him as he played with his favourite cars outside and some distance from the Hall. Over a period of time she gradually reduced the distance, moving nearer and nearer to the Hall doors. Eventually Simon felt comfortable going just inside the Hall. Finally, the support assistant substituted books for the cars.

Implement, monitor, evaluate

Having designed a programme of intervention with appropriate rewards, it is important to record and monitor outcomes. Change may be gradual or immediate, and unexpected effects may occur. It is important to be able to track why and how success occurs as well as to identify possible sources of difficulty so that accurate, targeted, alterations may be made to the programme. It is equally important to change only one element of a programme at a time.

Jon had been 'uncontrollable' in the teaching and therapy sessions at the Child Development Centre. The TEACCH approach was introduced, and Jon learned to recognise which activity came next by looking at the sequence of pictures on his board – taking each picture away when he had completed that item. Calm prevailed. After several weeks, however, the system broke down – as Jon insisted on taking the pictures from the board before even starting an activity.

His teacher wondered if the activities were now too easy for him, and she considered changing some of them. She tested this 'hypothesis' by changing just one activity – substituting a more complex toy for a simple marble game. During this activity, Jon left the picture on the board and became absorbed in the new task. This convinced his teacher that she had pinpointed the source of the difficulty. She went on to gradually introduce a range of more complex tasks.

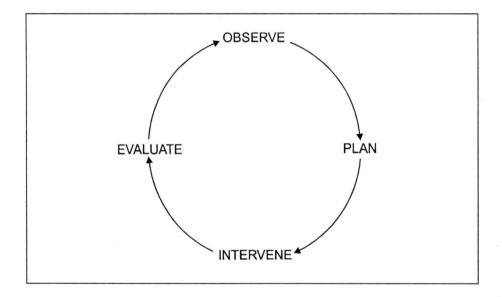

Figure 5.3 Planning cycle

Summary   When behaviour difficulties occur, intervene systematically, basing interventions on careful, informed, methodical observation and data collection.

- Make a plan of action.
- Identify positive behaviours, strengths and skills.

- Specify the purpose or function of the behaviour *for the child*.
- Define the nature of the difficult behaviours *precisely*.
- Complete careful observations and record *setting* conditions, *triggers* for behaviours, ensuing *actions* or events and the *results* or outcomes.
- Design the intervention programme, concentrating efforts on introducing, reinforcing and extending appropriate and desired behaviours, to bring about long-term improvements.
- Use graded change techniques.
- Relate rewards to the child: ensure they are meaningful, powerful, consistent and predictable.
- Consider using obsessional interests as reinforcers or rewards, as a way of introducing more acceptable behaviours and to increase desired skills.
- Monitor results – that is, keep recording!
- Evaluate outcomes against the original aims and redesign the programme if necessary.

Chapter 6

Towards Precision in Assessment and Teaching

Starting points

Once it has been established that Asperger syndrome is at the root of the child's difficulties, it is possible to extend our understanding of him. Initially it is all too easy to see only the difficulties and to be overwhelmed by them. It is necessary to establish a starting point for understanding and intervention. As one teacher said, 'I don't need any special equipment, I just need to understand Bethany in order to help her.'

Hans Asperger described these children as 'troublesome but fascinating'.

Observation leading to intervention

It is easy to lose sight of the child within the syndrome, particularly if he is a member of a large class group. It is only by observing children and reflecting on these observations that we begin to see and understand any situation. We make assumptions about children all the time. Careful observation, over a period of time, enables us to test these assumptions against the reality of the situation.

Following observations, a baseline can be established. Then it is possible to plan the way forward, putting into practice interventions designed to extend the experiences of the child and so facilitate his/her learning.

Profile

Use this profile format to help identify the child's particular areas of need within Asperger syndrome.

Part 1. Word picture
One head teacher summarised a ten-year-old boy in a mainstream class of 32 children under the following headings:

Part 1 Give a brief word picture of the child
• a very strange, bizarre, little guy; • he's unpredictable; • it's difficult to know when he's happy; • it's quite easy to see *when* he's distressed, but difficult to know *why* he's distressed; • he's slightly isolated.

This general summary gives a brief 'word picture' of the child. It is necessary to zoom in from the wide focus in order to find starting points for the planning of intervention. Children with Asperger syndrome share the same core difficulties, but each child displays these difficulties in an individual way.

Part 2. Observed behaviours

Part 2 of the profile itemises behaviours characteristic of Asperger syndrome. Not every child will display all the behaviours to the same extent. The profile gives the observer the opportunity to judge the extent to which the child's behaviours cause concern. For example:

Part 2 OBSERVED BEHAVIOURS					
1. Social interaction	**1**	**2**	**3**	**4**	**5**
a) ability to use gesture, body posture, facial expression and eye-to-eye gaze in 1:1 situations			✔		
b) ability to use gesture, body posture, facial expression and eye-to-eye gaze in group interaction					✔
c) ability to follow social cues in 1:1 with adults				✔	
d) ability to follow social cues in 1:1 with other children				✔	

Level of concern: 1 – No cause for concern
                        2 – Mild cause for concern
                        3 – Moderate cause for concern
                        4 – Serious cause for concern
                        5 – Great cause for concern					

In this example, the child's ability to use non-verbal communication in a group situation is causing great concern – although it is of less concern in one-to-one settings. His ability to follow social cues is also a major concern.

On completion of the profile, consideration should be given to the settings in which the child presents the greatest concern. It is then often possible to recognise a pattern, which, in turn, guides intervention.

Part 3. The response profile

To make interpretation of the results easier, the ticks are transferred to a colour-coded response profile. The areas causing greatest concern can then be identified at a glance. From this information, prioritise the three difficulties which are causing the greatest concern.

Part 4. Interpretation

At this point it will be useful to apply the 'Asperger lens' to the concerns which have been prioritised.

Use your understanding of Asperger syndrome to help identify the source of the child's difficulties. For example:

Part 4 Concerns	Possible sources
The child rarely gives eye-to-eye contact in 1:1 settings. He can't talk and look at the same time.	Difficulty in understanding non-verbal communication. Poor social skills.

Part 5. Intervention planning

At this stage, it is useful to bring together parents and professionals in order to compare views. This meeting should result in the production of an agreed intervention plan. For example:

Part 5	Intervention plan
Targets	**Strategies**
Child to be able to relate a sequence of 3 events.	1. Take photos of the child involved in the event. 2. Group the photos into sequences of three. 3. Get the child to reflect on what he did, then to put the photos in the correct order. 4. Let him use the photos as prompts as he relates what happened.

Evaluation

Set a period of time for the initial intervention. At the end of this period, use the schedule again to assess how the child's profile has changed, and the amount of progress which has been made.

The profile is not intended to be a diagnostic checklist. It is designed to give teachers information about a child's strengths and weaknesses within Asperger syndrome – and to provide starting points for intervention.

Observation profile

Part 1   Give a brief 'word picture' of the child within the class, noting positive points as well as difficulties.

Part 2   OBSERVED BEHAVIOURS

Key: 1   No cause for concern
2   Mild cause for concern
3   Moderate cause for concern
4   Serious cause for concern
5   Great cause for concern

1. Social interaction	1	2	3	4	5
a) ability to use gesture, body posture, facial expression and eye-to-eye gaze in 1:1 situation.					
b) ability to use gesture, body posture, facial expression and eye-to-eye gaze in group interaction.					
c) ability to follow social cues in 1:1 – with adults.					
d) ability to follow social cues in 1:1 – with other children.					
e) ability to follow social cues in group interaction.					
f) ability to share an activity with other children.					
g) ability to share an activity with an adult.					
h) ability to develop peer friendships.					
i) ability to seek comfort/affection when upset.					
j) ability to offer comfort/affection to others.					
k) ability to share in others' enjoyment/pleasure.					
l) ability to imitate other children.					
m) ability to imitate adults.					
n) ability to show different responses to different people in different situations.					
o) ability to respond appropriately to social praise.					
p) ability to respond appropriately to criticism.					

Comments

2. Social communication	1	2	3	4	5
a) ability to respond when called by name.					
b) ability to follow verbal instructions in 1:1 setting.					
c) ability to follow verbal instructions in a small group setting.					
d) ability to follow verbal instructions in a whole class setting.					
e) ability to take turns in conversations.					
f) ability to initiate conversation.					
g) ability to change topic of conversation.					
h) ability to maintain an appropriate conversation.					
i) ability to show awareness of the listener's needs.					
j) ability to give appropriate non-verbal signals as a listener.					
k) ability to change the topic or style of a conversation to suit the listener.					
l) ability to appropriately change the volume and tone of voice.					
m) ability to recognise and respond to non-verbal cues, eg: a frown.					
n) ability to understand implied meanings.					
o) ability to tell or write an imaginative story.					
p) ability to relate a sequence of events.					
q) ability to give a simple sequence of instructions.					

Comments

3. Social imagination and flexible thinking	1	2	3	4	5
a) ability to have varied interests.					
b) ability to share interests.					
c) ability to change behaviour according to the situation.					
d) ability to accept changes in rules, routines or procedures.					
e) ability to play imaginatively when alone.					
f) ability to play imaginatively together with others.					
g) ability to accept others' points of view.					
h) ability to generalise learning.					
i) ability to transfer skills across the curriculum.					
j) ability to plan an event or a task.					
k) ability to suggest possible explanations for events.					
l) ability to use inference and deduction.					

Comments

4. Motor and organisational skills	1	2	3	4	5
a) ability to find his way around the classroom.					
b) ability to find his way around the school.					
c) ability to sit still.					
d) ability to sit amongst a small group.					
e) ability to sit amongst a large group, eg: in assembly.					
f) ability to find and organise the equipment he needs for a given task.					
g) ability to write legibly and draw accurately.					
h) ability to get changed without help, eg: for PE.					
i) ability to organise his movements in PE and Games.					

Comments

Note the settings in which the child shows anxiety, stress or frustration.
EG: PE in the Hall / at transition times / sitting amongst a large group.

Prioritise the 3 difficulties which cause you the greatest concern

1

2

3

Part 3   RESPONSE PROFILE

Suggested colour key : 1 – Blue   2 – Green   3 – Yellow   4 – Orange   5 – Red

1. Social interaction

a) ability to use gesture etc, 1:1
b) ability to use gesture etc, in groups
c) ability to follow social cues 1:1 (adults)
d) ability to follow social cues 1:1 (children)
e) ability to follow social cues in a group
f) ability to share an activity – other children
g) ability to share an activity – adult
h) ability to develop peer friendships
i) ability to seek comfort/affection
j) ability to offer comfort/affection
k) ability to share in others' enjoyment
l) ability to imitate other children
m) ability to imitate adults
n) ability to show different responses
o) ability to respond appropriately to praise
p) ability to respond approp. to criticism

2. Social communication

a) ability to respond when called by name
b) ability to follow verbal instr. – 1:1
c) ability to follow verbal instr. – group
d) ability to follow verbal instr. – class
e) ability to take turns in conversations
f) ability to initiate conversations
g) ability to change topic of conversation
h) ability to maintain conversation
i) ability to show awareness of listener need
j) ability to give approp. non-verbal signals
k) ability to change style – to suit a listener
l) ability to change tone/volume of voice
m) ability to respond to non-verbal signals
n) ability to understand implied meanings
o) ability to tell/write an imaginative story
p) ability to relate a sequence of events
q) ability to give a sequence of instructions

3. Social imagination

a) ability to have varied interests
b) ability to share interests
c) ability to change behaviour in situation
d) ability to accept changes in routines etc
e) ability to play imaginatively alone
f) ability to play imaginatively with others
g) ability to accept others' point of view
h) ability to generalise learning
i) ability to transfer skills across curriculum
j) ability to plan an event or task
k) ability to suggest explanations
l) ability to use inference or deduction

4. Motor/organisation skills

a) ability to find way round classroom
b) ability to find way round school
c) ability to sit still
d) ability to sit amongst a small group
e) ability to sit amongst a large group
f) ability to find and organise equipment
g) ability to write legibly/draw accurately
h) ability to get changed without help
i) ability to organise movements in PE

Part 4	Concerns	Possible sources

Part 5	INTERVENTION PLAN	
Targets		**Strategies**

Appendix: Diagnostic Criteria for Asperger Syndrome

From: ICD 10 (World Health Organisation 1992)

A. *A lack of any clinically significant delay in language or cognitive development.*

   Diagnosis requires that single words should have developed by two years of age or earlier and that communicative phrases be used by three years of age or earlier. Self-help skills, adaptive behaviour and curiosity about the environment during the first three years should be at a level consistent with normal intellectual development. However, motor milestones may be somewhat delayed and motor clumsiness is usual (although not a necessary diagnostic feature). Isolated special skills, often related to abnormal preoccupations, are common, but are not required for diagnosis.

B. *Qualitative impairments in reciprocal social interaction (criteria as for autism).*

   Diagnosis requires demonstrable abnormalities in at least 3 out of the following 5 areas:

   1. failure adequately to use eye-to-eye gaze, facial expression, body posture and gesture to regulate social interaction;
   2. failure to develop (in a manner appropriate to mental age, and despite ample opportunities) peer relationships that involve a mutual sharing of interests, activities and emotions;
   3. rarely seeking and using other people for comfort and affection at times of stress or distress and/or offering comfort and affection to others when they are showing distress or unhappiness;
   4. lack of shared enjoyment in terms of vicarious pleasure in other people's happiness and/or a spontaneous seeking to share their own enjoyment through joint involvement with others;
   5. a lack of socio-emotional reciprocity as shown by an impaired or deviant response to other people's emotions; and/or lack of modulation of behaviour according to social context, and/or a weak integration of social, emotional and communicative behaviours.

C. *Restricted, repetitive and stereotyped patterns of behaviour, interests and activities.*

   (Criteria as for autism; however it would be less usual for these to include either motor mannerisms or preoccupations with part-objects or non-functional elements of play materials).

Diagnosis requires demonstrable abnormalities in at least 2 out of the following 6 areas:

1. an encompassing preoccupation with stereotyped and restricted patterns of interest;
2. specific attachments to unusual objects;
3. apparently compulsive adherence to specific, non-functional, routines or rituals;
4. stereotyped and repetitive motor mannerisms that involve either hand/finger flapping or twisting, or complex whole body movement;
5. preoccupations with part-objects or non-functional elements of play materials (such as their odour, the feel of their surface, or the noise/vibration that they generate);
6. distress over changes in small, non-functional, details of the environment.

D. *The disorder is not attributable to the other varieties of pervasive developmental disorder;* schizotypal disorder; simple schizophrenia; reactive and disinhibited attachment disorder of childhood; obsessional personality disorder; obsessive compulsive disorder.

From: DSM IV (American Psychiatric Association 1994)

A. *Qualitative impairment in social interaction as manifested by at least two of the following:*

1. marked impairment in the use of multiple non-verbal behaviours such as eye-to-eye gaze, facial expression, body postures and gestures to regulate social interaction.
2. failure to develop peer relationships appropriate to developmental level.
3. a lack of spontaneous seeking to share enjoyment, interests or achievements with other people (eg: by a lack of showing, bringing, or pointing out objects of interest to other people).
4. lack of social or emotional reciprocity.

B. *Restricted, repetitive and stereotyped patterns of behaviour, interests and activities, as manifested by at least one of the following:*

1. encompassing preoccupation with one or more stereotyped and restricted patterns of interest that is abnormal either in intensity or focus.
2. apparently inflexible adherence to specific, non-functional routines or rituals.
3. stereotyped and repetitive motor mannerisms (eg: hand or finger flapping or twisting, or complex whole body movements).
4. persistent preoccupation with parts of objects.

C. *The disturbance causes clinically significant impairment in social, occupational or other important areas of functioning.*

D. *There is no clinically significant general delay in language (eg: single words used by 2 years, communicative phrases used by age 3 years).*

E. *There is no clinically significant delay in cognitive development or in the development of age-appropriate self-help skills, adaptive behaviour (other than in social interaction), and curiosity about the environment in childhood.*

F. *Criteria are not met for another specific Pervasive Developmental Disorder or Schizophrenia.*

References

American Psychiatric Association (1987) *Diagnostic and Statistical Manual of Mental Disorders, 3rd edition – revised (DSM III-R)* Washington: American Psychiatric Association.

American Psychiatric Association (1994) *Diagnostic and Statistical Manual of Mental Disorders, 4th edition (DSM IV)* Washington: American Psychiatric Association.

Asperger, H. (1944) 'Die "autistischen Psychopathen" im Kindesalter', *Archiv fur Psychiatrie und Nervenkrankheiten* **117**, 76–136. English translation in Frith, U. (ed.) (1991).

Baron-Cohen, S. (1990) 'Autism: a specific cognitive disorder of "Mind Blindness"', *International Journal of Psychiatry* **2**, 81–90.

Baron-Cohen, S. (1996) *Mindblindness. An Essay on Autism and Theory of Mind*. Cambridge, Mass.: MIT Press.

Baron-Cohen, S., Leslie, A.M., Frith, U. (1985) 'Does the autistic child have a Theory of Mind?' *Cognition* **21**, 37–46.

Bleuler, E. (1911) *Dementia praecox oder gruppe der schizophrenien* (J. Zinkin translation 1950). New York: International University Press.

Ehlers, S. and Gillberg, C. (1993) 'The epidemiology of Asperger syndrome: a total population study', *Journal of Child Psychology and Psychiatry* **34**, 1327–1350.

Evans, G. (1997) 'The development of the outdoor education programme at Storm House School'. In: Powell, S. and Jordan, R., *Autism and Learning*. London: David Fulton.

Frith, U. (1989) *Autism, Explaining the Enigma*. Oxford: Basil Blackwell.

Frith, U. (ed.) (1991) *Autism and Asperger Syndrome*. Cambridge: Cambridge University Press.

Gillberg, C. (1989) 'Asperger syndrome in 23 Swedish children', *Developmental Medicine and Child Neurology* **31**, 520–531.

Gillberg, C. (1990) 'Autism and pervasive developmental disorders', *Journal of Child Psychology and Psychiatry* **31**, 99–119.

Gillberg, C. (1991) 'Clinical and neurobiological aspects of Asperger syndrome in 6 family studies'. In: Frith, U. (ed.), *Autism and Asperger Syndrome*. Cambridge: Cambridge University Press.

Gillberg, C. and Coleman, M. (1992) *The Biology of the Autistic Syndromes*. London: MacKeith.

Goldman-Rakic, P. (1987) 'Development of cortical circuitry and cognitive function', *Child Development* **58**, 601–622.

Grandin, T. and Scariano, M. (1986) *Emergence, Labelled Autistic*. Tunbridge Wells: Costello.

Green, J. (1990) 'Is Asperger's a syndrome?' *Developmental Medicine and Child Neurology* **32**, 743–747.

Happé, F. (1994) *Autism, an Introduction to Psychological Theory*. London: UCL Press.

Happé, F. and Frith, U. (1995) 'Theory of Mind in autism'. In: Schopler, E. and Mesibov, G. B. (eds), *Learning and Cognition in Autism*. New York: Plenum Press.

Hobson, P. (1993) *Autism and the Development of Mind*. Hove: Laurence Erlbaum.

Howlin, P. and Rutter, M. (1987) *Treatment of Autistic Children*. Chichester: John Wiley.

Jordan, R. and Powell, S. (1995) *Understanding and Teaching Children with Autism*. Chichester: John Wiley.

Kanner, L. (1943) 'Autistic disturbance of affective contact', *Nervous Child* **2**, 217–250.

Le Couteur, A., Rutter, M., Lord, C., Rios, P., Robertson, S., Holdgrafer, M., McLennan, J. (1989) 'Autism Diagnostic Interview: a standardised investigator-based instrument', *Journal of Autism and Developmental Disorders* **19**, 363–389.

Lord, C., Rutter, M., Goode, S., Heemsbergen, J., Jordan, H., Mawhood, L., Schopler, E. (1989). 'Autism Diagnostic Observation Schedule: a standardised observation of communicative and social behaviour', *Journal of Autism and Developmental Disorders* **19**, 185–197.

Luria, A.R. (1966) *The Higher Cortical Functions in Man*. New York: Basic Books.

Madsen, C.H., Becker, W.C., Thomas, D.R. (1968) 'Rules, praise and ignoring: elements of elementary classroom control', *Journal of Applied Behavioural Analysis* **1**, 139–150.

Newson, E. (1992) Enabling flexibility and social empathy in able autistic children: some practical strategies. Unpublished paper. Arhus Conference October 1992.

Ozonoff, S. (1995) 'Executive functions in autism'. In: Schopler, E. and Mesibov, G.B (eds), *Learning and Cognition in Autism*. New York: Plenum Press.

Peers, J. (1997) An Aspergee's guide to obsessions. Unpublished booklet.

Perner, J., Frith, U., Leslie, A.M., Leekham, S.R. (1989) 'Exploration of the autistic child's Theory of Mind: knowledge, belief and communication', *Child Development* **60**, 689–700.

Powell, S. and Jordan, R. (1997) *Autism and Learning*. London: David Fulton.

Rinaldi, W. (1992) *The Social Use of Language Programme*. Windsor: NFER – Nelson.

Rutter, M. (1978) 'Language disorder and infantile autism'. In: Rutter, M. and Schopler, E. (eds), *Autism: A Reappraisal of Concepts and Treatments*. New York: Plenum Press.

Schopler, E., Mesibov, G.B., Hearsey, K. (1995) 'Structured teaching in the TEACCH system'. In: Schopler, E. and Mesibov, G.B. (eds), *Learning and Cognition in Autism*. New York: Plenum Press.

Schopler, E., Reichler, R.J., Bashford, A., Lansing, M.D., Marcus, L.M. (1990). *Psychoeducational Profile – Revised (PEP-R)*. Austin, Texas: Pro-Ed.

Schopler, E., Reichler, R.J., DeVellis, R.F., Daily, K. (1980) 'Towards objective classification of childhood autism: Childhood Autism Rating Scale', *Journal of Autism and Developmental Disorders* **10**, 91–101.

Tantam, D. (1987) *A Mind of One's Own*. London: National Autistic Society.

Tantam, D. (1997) Unpublished paper.

Warnock Report (1978) *Special Educational Needs*. London: HMSO.

Wechsler, D. (1991) *Wechsler Intelligence Scale for Children (WISC)*. New York: Harcourt Brace Jovanovich.

Williams, D. (1996) *Autism: An Inside Out Approach*. London: Jessica Kingsley.

Wing, L. (1981a) 'Language, social and cognitive impairments in autism and severe mental retardation', *Journal of Autism and Developmental Disorders* **11**, 31–44.

Wing, L. (1981b) 'Asperger's syndrome: a clinical account', *Journal of Psychological Medicine* **11**, 115–129.

Wing, L. (1991) 'The relationship between Asperger's syndrome and Kanner's autism'. In: Frith, U. (ed.), *Autism and Asperger Syndrome*. Cambridge: Cambridge University Press.

Wing, L. (1996) *The Autistic Spectrum*. London: Constable.

Wing, L. and Gould, J. (1979) 'Severe impairments of social interaction and associated abnormalities in children: epidemiology and classification', *Journal of Autism and Childhood Schizophrenia* **9**, 11–29.

Witkin, H.A., Oltman, P.K., Roskin, E., Karp, S. (1971) *A Manual for the Embedded Figures Test*. California: Consulting Psychologists Press.

World Health Organisation (1978) *International Statistical Classification of Diseases and Related Health Problems*, 9th edition (ICD 9). Geneva: World Health Organisation.

World Health Organisation (1992) *International Statistical Classification of Diseases and Related Health Problems*, 10th edition (ICD 10). Geneva: World Health Organisation.

Zarkowska, E. and Clements, J. (1988) *Problem Behaviour in People with Severe Learning Difficulties*. Croom Helm: London.

Index